MW01592772

FROM CUFFS
TO
RECOVERY

FROM CUFFS
TO
RECOVERY

A COLLECTION OF INTERVIEWS WITH
MEN WHO BROKE FREE FROM ADDICTION

by

TJ S.

Copyright © 2022 TJ S.

All rights reserved.

No portion of this publication may be reproduced in any manner without the written permission of the publisher.

Library of Congress Control Number: 2022919790
ISBN-13: 979-8357110053

Printed in the United States of America

Dedication

To each of the men that shared their stories—
content for this book was made possible by
your courage, candidness, and trust.
I hope I've done justice to your voice.

Contents

Though wanted by the FBI, he knew he must clean up the wreckage of his past to keep the sobriety he had come to treasure.

This survivor fought hard to break free from repeated relapse into addiction. Yet, it was complete surrender that released him from its grip.

As a successful soldier, he felt entitled to his freedom. But in civilian life, consequences caught up with him and snatched that away.

Once homeless on the streets of Alaska, this self-made man proves that an atheist can thrive in Alcoholics Anonymous.

Author's Note

This publication is not Alcoholics Anonymous General Service Conference-approved literature. It does not imply any affiliation with or approval from Alcoholics Anonymous World Services, Inc. It does not endorse nor oppose any individual, recovery program, institution, organization, or creed.

This fact-based book is a collection of interviews, in which contributors tell their personal stories. Opinions expressed are those of the person who gave them. Recorded conversations were obtained via teleconferences, phone calls, texts, emails, and in-person meetings. Those were then transcribed. Material from follow-up Q&A sessions has been embedded in original content to achieve clarity and continuity. Because interviews totaled between two to six hours per contributor, portions were edited for brevity and relevance. Each chapter begins with a creative narrative, and one man wrote most of his story himself.

Throughout this book, the term "addiction" refers to both alcoholism and drug addiction. Some dates, names of people, and places have been changed or omitted to preserve anonymity. Contributors proofed only their respective chapters for accuracy, then granted their permission to print in this collection. They were not compensated in any way for their contribution. They simply wish to be of service.

INTRODUCTION

When I opened my eyes there was just one thought— "Fuck! Another fucking day! What's it gonna take to get through this day?" Then, I reached for my bottle and a joint. I was beaten—physically, mentally, emotionally, spiritually, and financially. Though I had cheated death ten times over, in the end, it was death I wished for. The men featured in this book have been there. Done that. Now, they describe their lives as being beyond their wildest dreams. I can agree.

Unlike them, I've not done hard time. But I *am* a survivor of trauma from living in active addiction—both my dad's and my own. On several occasions, SWAT visited my home. I crashed cars. I've lost a house, a fortune, and two marriages. Along the way, I've had to say too many goodbyes to family and friends. Some left in handcuffs, others in caskets. At one point in my journey, I was labeled a "hopeless case." That dude said that if I didn't get my shit together my fate would be jails, institutions, or death. If only he could see me now.

I met the guys in the following chapters through AA. Here, we talk about their path out of Hell and into freedom. I ask questions and they tell me their story—what it was like, what happened, and what it's like now. All is not a utopia for them and they're not saints. But they do enjoy life today and can look the world in the eye with integrity. In this book, they bare their battle scars to help others achieve what they have. Collectively, we aim to serve as a conduit to recovery.

addiction

[*uh*-**dik**-sh*uh*n]

noun

The state of being compulsively committed to a habit or practice, or to something that is psychologically or physically habit-forming to such an extent that its cessation causes severe trauma.

"Whatever I gotta do to pay off the drug dealer's car and make sure his wife has nice jewelry, I do it. That's just the nature of the beast."
—John

alcoholism

[**al**-k*uh*-haw-liz-*uh*m]

noun

An addiction to the consumption of alcoholic liquor or the mental illness and compulsive behavior resulting from alcohol dependency.

'Cause at the time, I'm just thinkin' of that next drink. You know? 'Cause when I'm drinking, all I can think of is— How can I get it? How can I get more? How long is it going to last? How am I going to cover it up?"
—Brad

Are You Done?!

*"I've been shot in the back, stabbed in the heart, and
overdosed on heroin twice!
What else can they do to me?!"*

Doug often announces that in meetings, and I roll my eyes every time he does. He talks about "crack hoes," and "titty dancers," causing everyone in the room to blush and shake their heads. He calls out people returning from relapses, "Are you done?!" Then he asks them again and again. Sharp. Loud. Clear.

For years, I saw him as a misogynistic braggart. Doug tells stories that are so far out there, they can't possibly be true, right? But now I get it. I know him better. Yes, Doug can be offensive, harsh, and vulgar at times. But I have to hand it to him—he's the most authentic, street-savvy person I know. And with fourteen years of sobriety, something's got to be working for him. He's not bragging. No. In fact, he's ashamed. But he's willing to share his experience, strength, and hope to help others like him.

Doug is my first interviewee. He agrees to tell me his story in its entirety—what it was like, what happened, and what it's like now. On this first day of our interview, he gives me a ride home from the club we frequent for AA meetings. But first, we swing by his house.

"I gotta let my dogs out," he says.

I picture Rottweilers as rough as he is, pit bulls, or something just as menacing. Yet when we arrive, two Shih Tzus greet us with wagging tails. We walk out to the backyard, where Doug throws a ball for them while showing me the shed he built. I would have never guessed it, but he's a carpentry virtuoso. His masterpiece is skillfully constructed and even includes a skylight.

"When did you learn carpentry?" I ask.

> "I started working young. I liked to build things. So, I became a carpenter and did that for thirty years. I also worked on bridges, built dams and high-rises. Shit, it's nothin' for me to walk backward on a steel beam seven-hundred and fifty feet in the air."

Back in his living room, we discuss the high prices of cable and Internet services. When I tell him I only have local channels due to the expense, he fires up his Roku TV.[1]

> "I got rid of cable… This has every channel you could possibly want. Hundreds… I bought it at Christmas time. A hundred and fifty bucks! Buy your own modem and you're set! My bill's down around fifty bucks a month now… Check out the clarity!"

It is, indeed, vivid. And mounted above it is a sweet soundbar. He selects a Christian rock concert and blasts it.

---

[1] Roku is a TV streaming platform that delivers audio and video content over the Internet.

"Look at the energy in that place!" He shouts while swaying and singing along.

I'm amazed. Before me stands a hard-core ex-biker rocking out to Christian music. There are more surprises to come.

Driving to my house, Doug shares his philosophy on negotiation.

"So, when I bought this truck, I was only gonna spend seven thousand… You know what gets people?" He rubs his fingers together. "Greed… See, I go to the bank and get stacks of brand new hundred-dollar bills. You know, with the thousand-dollar wrapper around them. Know what I mean?"

I have no idea. I've never held that kind of cash in my hand.

"I wasn't looking for anything fancy. Just a tool. A truck's nothin' but a tool to me, see. So, when I went to look at this truck, the guy's showin' me, and the whole time I'm checkin' it out, I've got that cash stickin' out of my shirt pocket. And I've got a stack in my hands and I'm doin' this."

In the air, he holds an invisible stack of cash. He bends it back by its band and riffles crisp bills with his thumb like a dealer would a deck of cards.

I see it. Hear it. Smell it. I imagine the impression it would make on anyone.

"The guy told me he wanted ten grand, and I just kept doin' this. 'Tell you what,' I said. 'I'll give you seven thousand right now. I got it right here.'" Doug pats his chest.

"The guy said he needed more, and I just said I didn't have time to haggle. I had other trucks to look at. I had a Dodge waitin' for me. I don't care what make it is. 'Cause you see, a truck's nothin' but a tool to me.

"So, the guy kept watchin' while I kept doin' this. And I started to walk off. 'Sorry,' I said. 'Gotta go. I got other things to do.'

"Then he said, 'Wait! Wait just a minute! Maybe we can work something out.'

"I said, 'Nah, I ain't got time. I've got other things to do... Other trucks to look at.' You know what got him? Greed. When you put cash in front of 'em, greed gets 'em. I buy everything like that.

"And you gotta have a backup plan. Gotta bank that money... See, some guys out on the rigs were buyin' brand new trucks, jackin' 'em way up in the air. They'd get everything top-of-the-line. Shit, they even had heated outside mirrors."

"You're a trip, Doug... You're really smart, though."

"I don't know about that. I may be good with money. Right now, I'm workin' on my second million. My first million went to the courts, bail bondsmen, lawyers, POs, dope, booze, hoes, restitution, programs I've been in…"

We get to my house and stop under a canopy of evergreens to smoke. He offers me a menthol and our interview begins.

"What was your home life like when you were growing up?"

"My mom died when I was five—She was killed by a drunk driver. So, my dad was left with us five kids—one, two, three, four, and five. I was the oldest. I have four sisters."

"Wow… That must've been tough."

"My dad was a heroin addict. We moved around a lot. He worked in construction, and we just followed the money. We were gypsies." Doug hacks hard between drags.

"He used to beat me like a man. He'd take my sisters by their hair and swing 'em around like ragdolls." Doug makes circles with his fist, as if stirring batter in a bowl.

"Damn…"

"Yeah, I used to take the blame for a lot of stuff they did."

For the next few minutes, Doug tells me about trivial antics, met with harsh discipline. "He'd line us all up, we'd be bendin' over the couch like this. And he'd just go down the line, whacking us all with a paddle. You know, the ones with a rubber ball attached."

Having heard parts of his checkered past, I'd always suspected Doug survived a tough childhood—I knew he'd been in and out of juvenile hall. Still, it's disturbing to watch him act out abusive scenarios.

"How do you think those early experiences influenced your choices as you grew older?"

"We're a product of our environment. It's called, 'learned behavior.' Shit, it was nothin' for everybody to be smoking dope and throwin' back booze at the Thanksgiving table." He pinches off the cherry of his cigarette and we go inside.

After introducing himself to my pups—who take an instant liking to him—Doug sits down at my kitchen table for a long talk.

"You've mentioned committing 'petty' crimes when you were young. What sort of things did you do?"

"Let's see, robbin', stealin' money from the church—ripped off the collection plate, coyoting—smugglin' illegals across the border. Shit like that… normal stuff kids do." He grins and chuckles. "There was no honor. No honor in our family."

"How old were you when your criminal life began?"

"I got my first felony when I was seventeen. Distribution, Sales, and Conspiracy. RICO. Look it up.[2] You see, that's what they do. They stack charges on you. And what's conspiracy? They can't prove anything... 'Ah, but we know you were thinking about it.' See, that's how they get you."

"How many felonies do you have?"

He holds up two fingers. "The second one was for Aggravated Assault with a Deadly Weapon and Attempted Murder... Drug-related, of course. That's when they sent me to Florence, Arizona—maximum security... See, we used to have firefights."

"What's a firefight?"

"Gun fights. We had our Uzis. Seven hundred rounds per minute. Thirty-two round clips duct-taped together. Israeli firearms. Hand grenades. Thompson machine guns... Yeah, we had some automatic weaponry.

"We were in a bar this one time—me and Big Ed. We called him that 'cause he was a huge dude. He looked like a Viking. I mean, he was six-six. Long blonde beard. He used to braid it. Huge guy...

---

[2] RICO stands for the Racketeer Influenced and Corrupt Organizations Act.

"Anyway, there's this dude sittin' at the bar, eye-fuckin' me. You know, staring me down in the mirror that's behind all the bottles. So, I went over to Big Ed... I said, 'Hey man, you see that guy over there? Somethin's up. I think he's a cop.'

"Big Ed went over to him. He leaned over the guy and said, 'Hey friend, what's your problem? Why you eye-fuckin' my friend, here?'

"The guy looked at me and said, 'You killed my brother.'

"Now, this dude tracked me down, all the way into Phoenix, Arizona. It'd been twenty years since the fight he was talking about.

"I said, 'Hey, a lot of shots were fired that night.'

"Then Big Ed said to him, 'Look friend, you're gonna have to leave.' And he did. He left on his own recognizance. Otherwise, Big Ed would have helped him out. That's how it was back then. You gotta remember, I'm an ol' hippie from the '60s."

As our conversation veers in all directions, I find myself repeatedly asking, "Where was this again?" Doug was locked up in Arizona, California, Utah, and Michigan.

"Let's talk about what prison was like for you. How much time have you done total—throughout your life?"

"Ten years. Four years straight time. I had another four comin', but we'll talk about that later. When I got out, I had ten years' probation."

"What's being in prison like?"

"Look man, you wanna know what prison's like? Go rent the movie *American Me*. That'll give you an idea."

"That's not what I want. I want your personal experience."

"Ok… Well… When you go in, there's three to four hours of processing. Then they put you in an eight-by-six observation unit on a forty-five-day hold to see what kind of animal you are. They wanna see how you'll react to the environment. It's all about them monitoring you for confinement and also suicide watch. People go crazy when their freedom is taken away, man. You hear that click and there ain't a key in your pocket… After that, they introduce you to the general population. They put you in the yard."

"Tell me about the yard. What was that like?"

"You better find your way into a gang real quick. You got the Aryan Brotherhood [AB] over here, the Peckerheads over here. You got the Mexican Mafia, the blacks, and the Asians. You gotta join one for protection. Gotta stay in the middle of the herd.

"So they put you in the yard with the general population and you're the new guy. It's a circus, and you're in the spotlight. Everybody's sizing you up, looking to see what you're made of. Then you got shot callers with their posses behind 'em."

"What's a shock collar?" It must be a slang term.

"No! A shot caller, S-H-O-T C-A-L-L-E-R... Those are the guys that call all the shots.

"So the first thing I did was go up to the biggest, baddest dude—that was the shot caller for the AB—I went up to him and I kicked him in the balls as hard as I could. The dude didn't even move. That's how I got this." Doug spits out a wired bottom denture.

"He punched me so hard, I fell flat on my back. Then he asked me if I knew who he was and I said, 'No!' He leaned over me and I spit blood in his face. I got my ass beat. But after that, nobody messed with me.

"Or you get a sponsor and he vouches for you. But it's blood in, blood out. So if he fucks up, both of you are going down. They put the green light on you. That works in prison AND on the outside. Look, you remember that warden? Got shot right at his front door. Pizza delivery. They can get anyone, anywhere."

"What's the 'green light'?"

"Open season. You're the hunted. Assassination."

"So, once you're in a normal cell, what's that like?"

"You ever heard of a blanket party?"

I shake my head. "What's that?"

"A beat down. With some guys, on their first night in the joint, the other prisoners throw a blanket party. That's where a bunch of dudes sneak into a new guy's cell at night when he's sleeping. They wrap the blanket over his head and beat the shit out of him."

"Where are the guards?"

"Man, the prisoners run the joint. Shit, as soon as you go in, they know everything about you—why you're there, how much money you came in with. I went in with twelve hundred dollars, and the first night they tried to extort me.

"Then, another time, when I was in Tent City, three dudes tried to take my bunk. I said, 'Nah man, this is my bunk.' See you're assigned bunks. Mine was K-15, Tent 2. I gave the guy an upper cut. Like this… That's the best way to knock 'em out, you know. That's why fighters like to use an upper cut. Anyway, he dropped to the floor and his two partners turned around and walked away. You gotta stand up for yourself, man.

Fear is weakness. And they test you. Either you're a man, a punk, or somebody's bitch."

"Tell me about rape."

"Know how they say you don't wanna drop the soap? I've seen guys bend over in the showers, a couple of dudes hold his arms up against the wall, and ten guys get their balls off. Gang rape. See, you're either prey or predator…

"Then there's bitches in there—they'll do anything for you. I've had guys offer to give me a blow job. Offer to do my laundry. Submissives. That's their power."

"Aren't the guards supposed to be watching at all times?"

"Nah, man. There's ways around it. That kind of shit goes down all the time. The COs have a routine. Like clockwork. And everybody knows it."

"What's the difference between a shank and a shiv?"

"Same thing. A homemade weapon. You know, you can make a weapon out of anything. You can take a roll of toilet paper and roll it real tight. Just roll and roll and keep rolling until you get a tight, sharp shiv. Think about it. All you've got is time on your hands. Plenty of time to scheme. The mind is like a squirrel cage. You're locked up. You're like a dog in a shelter. An animal…"

"You've said there's real evil in there—true possession."

"Evil is power. See, humans know right from wrong. Animals go by instinct… Guys in the joint take pride in being animals. And they wanna keep you in there, so you never wanna let 'em know your release date. They play mind games. They're just straight up evil dudes. Straight up mean and evil. That's the way they were wired in their brain. Fuckin' with somebody all the time just to do it. And you know, they're sick people—just like it tells us in that book.[3] Some are sicker than others."

"What about tattoos? I see guys with all kinds of prison tattoos. How do they get them?"

"It's so easy. You can almost make an appointment."

"What about drugs? I heard drugs are like currency—that they're easier to get on the inside than they are on the street."

"Yeah, you can get whatever you want—heroin, speed, pills, pot. Whatever you want. But in prison, you've gotta have your wits about you. Respect few, trust none."

"How do drugs get in there?"

"They keester it. That's what they call it. They stick it up their ass."

---

[3] This is a reference to the "Big Book," which is a common term for the book *Alcoholics Anonymous* published by Alcoholics Anonymous World Services, Inc.

"What about education?"

"A lot of the guys aren't educated. See here… 'I got a ninth-grade education… One and one is three…'" He touches his fingers. "One and one is three. See?"

"Are you joking? You have a ninth-grade education?"

"No, no! I graduated from high school, 3.5. I had to go back to school because they kicked me out in 1970, 'cause I was a member of the SDS and the White Panthers. John Sinclair. SDS—Students for Democratic Society—they're a radical group. And also, I ran with the White Panthers out of Fenton, Michigan.

"So, they busted me with a quarter pound of weed in my locker in high school. So I said, 'Screw you!' I went and took night courses and graduated. 'Cause I was very adamant about getting my high school diploma. And that was in 1970. It was '72 when I graduated. Showed them all. 'Fuck you! Read this!'"

"Aren't some of the guys in penitentiaries self-educated? Don't they have access to books?"

"Yeah, and you can get time in the library for good behavior."

"Seems like you'd have all the time to learn anything. Why is it so many don't make it on the outside?"

"Some of the guys in there become institutionalized. They can't be rehabilitated. They can't make it on the outside 'cause they miss that routine. And look, they don't need to become taxpayers. Shit, they got a cot, shelter, food. They need that structure. That routine. That discipline. That's all they know. They become robots.

"And most of those guys bounced in and out of juvie hall. You know what you learn there? You learn about all your mistakes and how to fine-tune things when you get out. 'Let's see, should I wear cotton gloves or latex gloves next time?' You learn from the other prisoners. That's where you get educated.

"I'll tell you about the system… Arraignment. There we are, all in our DOC uniforms, waiting for our turn. And this dude goes up and the judge has his jacket in front of him. The kid was there for shoplifting. So, the judge asks the kid to tell him why he did it.

"He says, 'I was hungry… I took two twinkies and ate one while I was walking around, and then I decided to put the other one back.'

"The judge looked down at his jacket. You know, it shows how long you've been in there. That kid had been held for forty-five days waiting for a bail bond hearing. You're supposed to get an arraignment within seventy-two hours, see. Can you dig that, man?

"Let's go take a smoke break."

We go back outside and have a cigarette while bees bother us. Doug tells me about Tent City.

"Then they sent me to Maricopa County, Arizona. Joe Arpaio—toughest Sheriff in the West. Look it up. They give you pink clothes, pink underwear. Even your flip-flops are pink. And I used to fuck with all them inmates in there. I'd go and grab them guys by their collar and put it up by their eyes. I'd say, 'Man, that color pink sure brings out the color of your eyes.' Fuck with 'em all...

"You got one wool blanket. Slept in your clothes in the wintertime. In the summertime—imagine livin' outside in a hundred and fifteen plus. There used to be a big, bright neon sign way out in the desert that said, 'VACANCY.' You could see it from the road."

At this point, I've done some research. "It's closed now," I said.

"Yeah, 'cause we gotta have human rights. Gotta be nice to convicts. Yeah, totally raped your daughter and killed your wife…

"Man, I used to smuggle in a gram of cocaine every night. You know baseball caps, how they have that rim around 'em? You can take a gram in a little baggie and tuck it up under there. Then, when you go in, they have you toss all your things to the side. I'd just take off my hat and throw it in the pile with my socks. You pull out your pockets like this…"

"Was that while you were on work release?"

"Yeah… Twelve in, twelve out, every day. They came and checked on your job, make sure you were there. You never cashed your paycheck when you got it on Friday. You took that paycheck to the jailer. The clerk. And they charged you three dollars a day—back in the eighties—for your room. Then, we'd smoke pot. We'd turn on all the showers. Steam would hide the smoke."

"How did you get away with all that?"

"It's easy. You run interference. You get a couple guys, start a little fight over there. And the guards focus on that shit. You have guys—they're your watchers, you know—lookouts. Always something to distract 'em. You know? A lot of times guards are doing paperwork... or watching porn."

"Tell me about supermax facilities… You've said you worked on three in Maricopa, Arizona."

"Off Interstate 10, heading south. We built them from the ground up. Overcrowding for guys from Alaska, Hawaii, and

California. We were in the construction phase. Ground up. And what they do is, they go up like tilt-ups. They're all concrete. Four cells at a time, all poured in place—shitters, sinks. Everything. Beds. Concrete everything. They bring 'em out on flatbed semis. Pick 'em up with a crane. Just like Legos—stack 'em on top of each other. All that plumbing. Everything is all designed to go down the same. So, you could put a whole prison up within two weeks. All prefab. All concrete."

"Did you ever do time in one?"

"That's when I told my boss. I said, 'If I don't straighten my shit up, one of these rooms has got my name on it.'"

"When was that? That you worked on those?"

"That was back in the '80s."

"OK… I'm getting confused. What's the timeline?"

"I've worked all over the United States. The only years I can really recall—is that I was in Sacramento, California from 1990 to 1995 doin' tilt-up buildings, runnin' with the Hell's Angels. Dealin' speed. Taxman—tax collector. The rest, I was runnin' and gunnin' the whole time in Phoenix.

"Built most of the high rises down off of Central, Washington, Van Buren, Indian School, Thomas Earl, Camelback, it goes all the way up. The last high rise I did was in 2006, forty-four stories. Downtown Phoenix. A lot of the bridges on the 101

Freeway, the 202 Freeway, and the 303 Freeway. Red Mountain Pass over Tempe. That's all I did was construction. Superintendent and foreman—most of the jobs.

"I traveled all over the country for work. It was nothin'. I'd throw two bags in the truck and go. All I had were those bags and the toolbox in the back of my truck. They'd call me from all over, wanting me to go here and there. 'Cause I took pride in my work. And I was clean and sober. So, I went. Chasin' the money. I banked all of it. Shit, I'd eat for less than ten bucks a day. At one of my jobs, the payroll lady called me up and told me I needed to go open a bank account to cash the ten checks I had in my wallet. She needed to balance the books."

"How did you get sober?"

"I went to court, and I was given a choice. I could either go to a ninety-day rehab or go back and do four more years. I went to the rehab. Military-style. Only three percent make it. Shit, I could do ninety days standin' on my head."

"Had you ever tried to stop on your own?"

"Hell, no! Shit, when I went in, I was already plannin' my relapse. I wasn't done."

"Did you go in and out or did you stay?"

"I've never relapsed. When I was in rehabilitation—right after two weeks in there—they asked me to teach relapse prevention classes. Everybody had assignments."

"So, did you actually do the relapse prevention classes?"

"Yeah, I taught it! I had to go to school eight months afterward to be a drug relapse prevention counselor. But with my crazy mind, I wouldn't show you—how to prevent you from doing drugs. See, I'm an ol' hippie from the '60s. I'll show you how to do them correctly. 'Cause, there is no such thing as drug abuse. You hear it all the time—drug abuse. There is no such thing as drug abuse. You cannot abuse good drugs. You use them to the fullest potential! You can't abuse good drugs! I never did! I used 'em, and more. So, there is no such thing as drug abuse for me. I just couldn't get enough. So, you gotta be done, man. That's it."

"So, what was the shift? When were you were like, 'OK, I'm done!'? What happened?"

"We had to do meetings every day, K… They had meetings within walking distance. So, everybody had a piece of paper—a ninety-day sheet. Had to be signed by the person, and their phone number, and what the topic was. So, I was doing meetings, 'cause it was a requirement to be in there. And that's part of your recovery.

"So, when I asked that oldtimer—I had like two weeks in—to be my sponsor, that's when he got in my face and pointed his finger in my chest and said, 'Are you done? Are you done dopin' and drinkin'? Get honest in your heart, not your mind.'

"Because your mind will lie to you. It will minimize, rationalize, self-entitlement, expectations, instant gratification, the list goes on and on and on.

"He said, 'Look at your track record. What have you been doing? You haven't. So, you need to get honest—and that you're done, and you wanna live. And you'll be okay. But till you do your ninety meetings in ninety days, I don't have time for you. There's people out there that need this program—not want—need. So, you come back and talk to me after you do your ninety meetings in ninety days. And I want to see that paper signed 'cause I will check your shit.'"

"Was that your first sponsor?"

"Yep. Same one I still have. Fourteen years… Yep… So, I've never relapsed. 'Cause I've been done. People wanna say that maybe that's a resentment—that I hold against him, 'cause he got my face pointing his finger in my chest. Like, very threatening. No. He made me realize—you want to live or die… It's your choice.

"So, I've always remembered that. And that's what I live by. Are you done dopin' and drinkin'? And wanna live? Get honest with yourself. And that's what the program[4] taught me. Honest program. Do I lie and steal? And rob anymore? No. Lie like a mother fucker, 'cause I'm lie'n right now!" We laugh. "And what's the difference between a little lie, a white lie, and a big fat black lie? There is no difference. A lie is a lie is a lie. It doesn't matter, right? I try to do better."

"Yes, me too… OK, you wanna tell me about your on-the-run time?"

"Four years. From '07 to 2012. Four years wanted by the FBI for crossing Interstate lines to avoid prosecution and two felonies. I got busted for my second offense driving with no driver's license, 'cause they took my license for ten years. That never stopped me from driving. I didn't have a license, but I had to go to work. So, I got picked up for driving without a license.

"When I sat down with my PO, she told me she was gonna violate me. My jacket was this thick." With his fingers, Doug gestures about three and a half inches.

"They called me a habitual offender. They were going to send me back to prison for driving without a license. I'm going back

---

[4] This is a reference to the program of Alcoholics Anonymous.

to Florence, maximum-security prison in Florence, Arizona. And I said, 'OK, how does it work?'

"She looked at her big calendar on the desk and said, 'In two weeks we're gonna come. I'll bring up DOC—an officer from DOC—and the Phoenix Police Department to come and arrest you. And you will be taken down and processed. And you will go back and finish out your four years' time. You will not get good time served.'

"So, I said, 'OK. When are you coming to my house to arrest me so I can get all my affairs in order? Get rid of my dog, have somebody take care of my house—all these things I need. Which, I appreciate you not arresting me and taking me at the moment.' She named a date that was fourteen days away. I said 'OK, I will be at my house at 8:30 in the morning. When you come, I'll be ready to go.'

"So, I went home right after that meeting. Immediately. Started packing my truck. Went and got my sister. Pulled my plates off my truck. Registration in her name. That way when I'm traveling, they run them plates, I don't come up hot. It's clean. Somebody owns that other vehicle.

"Packed my shit. I had a big yard sale over the weekend. I put big flyers out on the corners. 'Estate sale—everything must go.' People came from all over. I made like, three thousand dollars Saturday and Sunday. I sold a new washing machine, dryer, refrigerator, can lights, ceiling fans, mirrored double wall closets—that you have in master bedrooms. Everything. I told them if they wanted the paint off the walls, scrape it. You can take it. Packed my shit and took off. To Florida. Called my cousin. Said, 'I'm coming down. I'm gonna be on the lam for a while. Need a place to lay low till I get my shit together. I got money.' I had about twenty grand in my pocket.

"So, I drove only at night. I was like a leaf in the wind. Got to Florida. Took the plates—Arizona plates—off my truck. Put it in my cousin's name. Now, I blend in. Under the radar. All I did is go to meetings and work. Stayed in the program. Traveled all over this United States—North Dakota, Bismarck to Port St. Lucie, Florida. All over Texas, Oklahoma, California. All over—building cooling towers on power plants.

"In 2012 on my way to Sturgis, South Dakota for the motorcycle rally. Called up the head cheese in Arizona Probation Department. Said, 'Hey man, my name is so and so. Here's my social. Run me. I'm coming in. I'm flying into Phoenix next week. I'm tired of runnin'. I've been in 12 Step recovery for five years. Haven't had no problems. I work with others, sponsor, do my meetings. I'm tired of running and I'm gonna go turn myself in.'

"The dude says he just picked up a twelve-year chip. So, him and I started talking about the program. And he got off onto a tangent for about ten minutes and then he caught himself. Got back to business. He said, 'Well, you got a couple of black marks here and that's running and the FBI warrants. But you got a good mark, you wanna turn yourself in and clean up the wreckage of your past.' He says, 'I cannot promise you anything. I can make recommendations to the judge. We want to clear the books of you. We want to clear these cases up. You send me one thousand eighty-five dollars overnight. Money order. FedEx. And I'll start processing your paperwork. No promises. Call me in three days.'

"I called back in three days. He said, 'The judge signed off and squashed the warrants. With stipulations.'

"And I said, 'OK, whatever the stipulations are, I'll do it.'

"He said, 'You can't come back to Arizona for five years.'

"I said, 'That's no problem.'

"He said, 'OK, cool. And we just want you to clear up this case. We want to clear this case up. We want clear books.' You know? Just like they do in other cases. They want to solve them. Put them away. Concentrate on the next one.

"I said, 'OK, cool… But what about my driver's license? I haven't had a driver's license in ten years.'

"He says, 'I am punched into the Motor Vehicle Department of Arizona. Your one thousand eighty-five dollars is for processing this paperwork. I'll punch it in. Call me back in three days.'

"Three days passed. I called him back. He says, 'You can come to Arizona for a few days, get your driver's license, and then you have to leave.'

"I said, 'Really? You'd do that for me?'

"He says, 'Yes.' The guy was really cool.

"So, I call up my partners, 'cause I rode Harley-Davidsons with a lot of bikers back there. Call up my partners. My old thinking came back, I say, 'Hey man, I'm coming back for a week. See you guys.'

"'OK, Doug… The Budweiser truck—keg truck—is parked in the driveway. The ounce of meth is lined up, and the titty dancers are here waiting. When you comin'? We'll pick you up at Sky Harbor Airport.'

"I says, 'Well you can pick me up, but I can't do that shit.'

"So I went, got my driver's license. And the thing was, an Arizona driver's license has a picture in the background of the Grand Canyon. All the Grand Canyon was there. All my license information was from a different state. Because I was under the jurisdiction of the state of Arizona for one year, I could not even get a parking ticket or the whole deal was off. Talk about walking a fine line. A tightrope. This was like in the pirate days—walking the plank. But you stopped at the end. You had a choice. You know, the saber in the back to keep going, or you straighten up and fly right. And that's what happened.

"And that was in 2012. No driver's license for ten years. Now, I have a CDL, Class A, tanker endorsement, and a hazmat. And it's all because of the grace of God and the program. Just work the program. That's what you gotta do. Keep it simple."

"What do you do for your program today?"

"I stay in the middle of the herd. That is—doing meetings, working with others. Whatever I can do."

"Do you sponsor people?"

"Two of 'em. I have two sponsees in Arizona. I've been asked to sponsor here, but I don't like to get overwhelmed. So, I don't overextend myself. I got enough problems with the two sponsees in Arizona comin' and goin'. They're not done. And I keep tellin' 'em, 'Well, your mom's got my address. She can

27

send me an obituary when you bite it. And then I put you with the rest of 'em. Oh, and by the way, we do play the Queen song at your funeral. And you know what it is—Another One Bites the Dust… Another one bites the dust! Another one bites the dust!" *Thump! Thump!* Doug smacks the table.

"Yeah, no mercy. You got a choice, man. You're in the middle. You make the choice. Dope and booze in the left hand, sobriety in the right. You make the choice. I'm real hard-core about that. And I don't sugarcoat nothin'. But it all comes down to being done.

"A preacher can tell you as much as he wants—repeat the same thing over and over again. And I've had people tell me, 'Doug, that's all you preach. Are you done? Are you done? Are you done dopin' and drinkin' and you wanna live?' Well, it works for me. Everybody has a choice. And the funny thing is, since I have sobriety—I have freedom to make that choice. Have I thought about relapse? Oh yeah, those crazy thoughts come in my head about the old days. You know? Being a cocaine dealer and speed dealer. We got an old sayin', 'Pack their nose and pack their hoes!'

"I'd walk into a party, throw out an ounce of meth or coke on the table and shower down. That's my teaser for everybody. The rest of the shit's bagged up in grams outside. I'll spend an ounce just for the party, just to get 'em teased. And then they're all breaking out their wallets or going to the ATM getting cash. They want some more. So, I can burn an ounce. That ain't shit. 'Cause the customers are right there... And that's what I used to do. Those are the days of my past… I've changed. I could go into war stories. You know? But now it's all about the program and that's all I can really say."

"Just a couple of things to clarify. When you were given the choice in rehab—either you work on the chain gang, or you go and get a job…"

"I had a job. I never worked on there. Guys on the chain gang were paid minimum wage, and I think it was like seven-eighty-five back in '07. Work in the heat all day—a hundred and fifteen plus. Chained up six feet apart, working on the freeways, picking up trash. Ten, twelve hours a day, six days a week.

"Know what I used to do when I got out? I'd go down the freeway, start honking my horn. You see the whole line of 'em. I'd scream out, 'Bob! Bob!' And wave. Well out of twenty guys, somebody's gotta be named Bob. So, it messed with their heads. 'Who was that? I know that guy!' Think about it. I used to fuck with them all…"

"So, you're obviously a Christian now."

"I always have been. I grew up Southern Baptist. Hellfire 'n' Brimstone. My sisters and I—we sang in the church choir growing up. And then when they get to the collection plate—

put it in the backroom—I went back there and ripped them envelopes open. Stole all that money. Take the two, three dollars, five dollars. Whatever. I did that. I wasn't even a teenager. Criminal activity... And I'm not bragging. I'm ashamed of a bunch of shit I did because of the choices I made. The lowest. 'Learned environment.' Where I grew up, we didn't care. Smoke pot after dinner."

"Do you think it's possible for people that are in prison—right now—to practice the principles of the program?"[5]

"To survive in prison, you have to be in prison. That's where you're at. In the free world, you have choices. There, you don't. Oh, you have a choice... and they'll green light you. You know, a guy will walk up and put a shiv in you and cut your throat. In the artery. In the neck. That's where I always went—for the neck.

"Like the guy who stabbed me in the heart. I pulled that knife out, went and got him in the neck. And then I went to lockdown for three days because I used excessive force. Even though he stabbed me in the heart, and I pulled the knife out. I retaliated."

"So, is it possible?"

---

[5] The twelve spiritual principles of Alcoholics Anonymous are: honesty, hope, faith, courage, integrity, willingness, humility, brotherly love, discipline, perseverance, spirituality, and service—as discussed in *The Twelve Steps and Twelve Traditions*, published by Alcoholics Anonymous World Services, Inc.

"It's possible. But all the guys that I ran with, that I knew—all they were doin'—you learn, you trade your experiences. 'I did it a million times. But I only got caught once.' And all convicts are innocent. 'But I did it a million times… But I got caught once.' So, you sharpen your skills in there. Try this, try that.

"But it's all about recovery. And it's all the choice you wanna make. You gotta quit runnin' and gunnin' with the people in your life. Think about it... Dope fiends, liars, and thieves run with dope fiends, liars, and thieves. Christians run with Christians. Alcoholics hang out in bars with other alcoholics. You're known by association. You gotta close that door and turn out that light switch and walk away. And that's a hard thing to do for a lot of people because of family, friends they've runned and gunned with all their lives.

"You know, you go to a kegger at the beach, they're all smokin' dope, pounding the big titted blonde—poundin' sand up her ass over there behind the bush. Whatever. Everybody knows everybody. This is what we do. We've done that every week, you know?

"So, you gotta—like I say—you gotta turn off that light and slam that door. And find other people that are like-minded. If you want sobriety... If you wanna live."

His Drug of Choice Was, "More!"

"It seemed like every drug I tried; I fell in love with."

With COVID came the birth of Zoom teleconference meetings.[6] This brought me a chance to get to know people from many different parts of the country—people I'd not otherwise be able to meet. That's how I've come to know and respect Chris—a charismatic character, to whom people are drawn. He's not easy to forget. Sometimes he reminds me, "Every day, I'm either working on a relapse or I'm working on recovery." From what I've observed, he walks the walk. Though a considerable part of his struggle has been with drugs, and he'll say that at one time he was a "junkie," he feels most at home in AA.

Chris allows me to interview him and is open to all my questions. But he keeps saying, "Yeah, this is all in my story." Or "I'll send you what I wrote. I cover this in my story." So, some of what is included here comes from a document he emailed to me after our first interview. As part of his recovery at a residential drug and alcohol treatment center, he wrote out his history in preparation for a speaker meeting. Thus, what follows is a blend of interview material, along with original writing and some paraphrasing.

---

[6] Zoom is an Internet communications platform that allows users to connect with video, audio, phone, and chat. It was developed by Zoom Video Communications, Inc.

Chris starts by telling me how he learned to cope by drinking and using early in his life. At twelve years of age, he had his first sip of alcohol and began smoking marijuana.

> "I had a low tolerance for reality. Life was boring, and I became addicted to feeling different… I was always attracted to breaking the rules."

His youth was somewhat ordinary. At five years of age, he survived his parents' "nasty" divorce. It was then that his father left the family. But before that, Chris endured a tumultuous home.

> "I recall one incident, in particular, when my dad locked himself in our downstairs bathroom with his .45 [handgun]. I remember him yelling, 'I'm gonna blow my fucking brains out!' through the bathroom door as my mom, my two older brothers, and I stood fearfully close by."

Growing up left Chris with lasting scars. Many arrests, multiple felony charges, and five stays in drug and alcohol treatment centers can attest to that. Not only was he a victim of childhood trauma, but he was also plagued by addiction and alcoholism, which seems to come with a self-destructive streak.

With his father gone, Chris looked to his two older brothers for male role models. He and Sam, six years his elder, were inseparable from the beginning.

Chris still remembers his mom saying that when he was born, Sam asked her, "Can I have him?"

"He wanted me all to himself. Not only did I idolize my brother, he was absolutely my best friend."

During our interview, Chris and I discuss how his alcoholic/addict career began. He maintains that early on, his life was typical.

"My elementary years were pretty normal—whatever normal is. I did good in school, played little league baseball…"

Summers were spent visiting family in Texas, near the Texas-Mexico border.

Chris wrote that at thirteen, he would—

"…sneak over to Mexico to purchase illegal fireworks, switchblades, or have the occasional Margarita."

"What other sorts of trouble did you find during those years?" I ask.

"Me and my friends would do stupid things, like tip over Porta Pottys, or steal clothes, but nothing major."

However, Chris was indeed following the path of his role models—one of which was stealing cars and motorcycles.

Unlike most older brothers, Sam and Michael (Michael being the eldest) took Chris with them when they went to kegger parties, where he was provided drugs and alcohol. He felt set apart from his peers and became a daredevil.

"I got to compete in the first-ever X Games as an amateur. I didn't place or anything, but I remember being on the local news and thinking I was hot shit."

Soon, poor choices brought serious consequences. Later that year, Chris visited a friend and accepted a childish dare.

"He dared me to jump off his second-story balcony and onto a pile of pillows we had collected from his mom's bed. So, I did—and I broke my back. This was when I was first introduced to painkillers. I'll never forget that warm fuzzy feeling my first Hydrocodone gave me."

Teenage years were full of love, experimentation, and unfortunately, further trauma. In his writing, Chris explains how middle school was, "pretty uneventful." He received average grades, mostly because—

"School wasn't that interesting. I was into girls, smoking weed, and the occasional beer or painkiller."

Then as a freshman, Chris met his first serious girlfriend, Sydney. They would be together for the next seven years. During that time, marijuana proved to be a gateway drug. Experimentation led to mushrooms, then LSD. Not only did he do further street research with hallucinogens, but Chris also toyed with highly potent stimulants.

"I'll never forget that first line of coke. I was transformed... I was sixteen."

Obtaining employment came easy to Chris. However, he struggled with responsibility. His first job as a clerk at a local convenience store allowed him access to alcohol and tobacco, which won him popularity.

> "Naturally, I soon became 'The Spot,' for fellow friends and high schoolers to purchase beer and cigarettes."

That job didn't last long, and neither did those that followed. His drug and alcohol use compromised his work ethic and performance.

> "I bet I had twenty different jobs when I was in high school."

At seventeen, the stakes grew higher for Chris. His brother, Sam, taught him how to find and purchase prescription drugs in Mexico. Selling narcotics became his next vocation.

> "We could go practically into any pharmacy and purchase Valium, Xanax, Roofies [Rohypnol], steroids, Adderall, or basically anything you wanted. We would hit various border towns. It wasn't long before I was smuggling hundreds of pills across various borders and bringing them back to Texas to sell."

Chris writes that at this point, his father resurfaced only to encourage poor decision making and substance abuse. They drank and did lines of cocaine together.

> "Around this time, my dad had decided to reappear and attempt to make a presence in my life. He attempted to do so by buying me a new pick-up truck and allowing me to host keg parties

with my friends at his trailer home. We would trade pills with one another and funnel beers around bonfires in his back pasture. This was how he made his amends for being absent all those years."

Life changed forever during the summer before Chris's senior year when his brother, Sam, died of a heroin overdose—only two days after celebrating his twenty-third birthday.

"That was a day I'll never forget. I was asleep upstairs at my mom's house when the doorbell rang at about two in the morning. I woke up and walked downstairs to the front door. My mom met me there in her nightgown. She answered the door. Two uniformed police officers were standing on our front porch. My mom turned and looked at me and asked, 'What have you done now?'

"I began to ask myself that same question… And then I heard it. The police officer informed us that my brother, Sam, was found dead in the bathroom of the filling station. I went completely numb. I had just lost my brother and my best friend. Nothing else seemed to matter. How in the hell was I supposed to start my last year of high school on the brink of such news?!"

At that moment, Chris swore he'd never do drugs again. But within weeks, he was loaded. His senior year was a fog, as he escaped from emotional pain with substances.

"I barely went to school. And when I did, I was messed up. If I didn't skip class that day, I smoked as much weed as possible or swallowed as many pills as I could put down before I went. I had missed so much school that my teachers and principals were calling the house to tell my mom I wasn't going to graduate."

Though Chris has struggled with addiction, he is intelligent and headstrong. Determined to graduate with his high school class, he pulled out all the stops.

"I began making up hours every chance I got. Going in before school, staying after, going in for eight hours on Saturdays—whatever I could do. Low and behold, I did manage to graduate on time. I'm still not quite sure how I managed to pull it all together, but I did."

After graduation, on his eighteenth birthday, Chris received a twenty-thousand-dollar check from the family business. As expected, he blew it on drugs. He resumed selling, and problems with law enforcement ensued.

"I was holding down a job as a front, but my main source of income was drugs. Although I must say, I was probably one of the worst drug dealers ever. I used way more than I sold. I had been living on my own for three whole months before I was faced with legal charges."

During our interview, Chris acknowledges that while he didn't always get into trouble when he drank and used, when he did get into trouble, drugs and alcohol were always involved.

> "I was busted—just outside of Mexico. The customs agents caught me smuggling nine hundred Valiums through the checkpoint. For the life of me, I don't know how or why, but they let me go—with the understanding, of course, that I would never step foot back into Mexico."

A short while later, Chris's house was raided, and he was charged with his first felony offense—Distribution of Marijuana. He was sentenced to fifteen days in county jail, three hundred hours of community service, and four years of probation. But his troubles were just beginning.

> "I was about two years into my probation when one night I was pulled over for running a stop sign. Of course, the officer asked to search. And since I didn't have anything to hide—I let him. After tearing my truck apart for about forty-five minutes, he finally came back to the cruiser and informed me I was being arrested. He held out his hand, and inside he had a single weed stem. I was arrested and charged with Possession of Marijuana—less than a gram! Gotta love Texas!"

Chris had violated his probation and that single weed stem sent him back to county jail for six months.

At twenty-two, life for Chris seemed to settle. He and Sydney rented a house on a lake. But now off probation, his drug use was back on.

"This is about the time I was first introduced to methamphetamine. I began to search different avenues for drug connections. It wasn't long before I discovered the 'Pill Farms.' Crooked doctor shops and pharmacies were popping up all over East Texas. If you had a valid ID, you could walk into any of these clinics and pick up 'the cocktail'—a pharmaceutical mix of three different scripts: Xanax, Soma, and Vicodin/Lortab or Oxycodone—depending on where you went.

"So now, instead of taking weekend trips to Mexico, my friends and I would head out to Houston for the weekend and stock up. Even my dad got in on the hustle. If we did it right, we could each hit three clinics and come back with thousands of pills on any given day. And since a lot of these off-grid pain clinics also owned their own pharmacies, there were no actual records kept in their national database, or DEA watch, limiting the number of prescriptions we could fill. The only drawback was that you could only hit each clinic once a month. Fortunately, I had a list of twenty different clinics I was using. Again, I was a shitty dealer, and it wasn't long before I was eating way more pills than I sold."

Sydney had had enough, and Chris was devastated when his first true love left him. Having never learned healthy coping skills, he stayed stoned.

41

"Xanax worked wonders."

Soon after, Chris was robbed at gunpoint.

> "Instead of giving the guy what he wanted, I hit him with a cane. I guess I tried to knock the gun out of his hand, but that isn't quite what happened. As soon as I noticed my attempt to disarm him hadn't quite panned out, I dove under a parked car. He pointed his gun at me and shot three times. Somehow, he missed, and just hit the pavement nearby. [When the cops arrived] I tried to tell them what happened, but they weren't hearing it. I didn't know this, but during the altercation, I had broken the guy's other arm with my cane. And he ditched the gun."

Chris was arrested and charged with Aggravated Assault with a Deadly Weapon—a second-degree felony. He was able to post bond but was still drowning in active addiction.

> "This was one of the lowest points in my life, right next to the night my brother died. My long-time high school sweetheart had just dumped me, I had just been fired from my job—and of course, I had just completed felony probation—and now here I was facing yet another felony. And just when I thought things couldn't get any worse, my world once again came crashing down on top of me."

Shortly afterward, Chris was driving while intoxicated when he nearly killed a thirty-five-year-old man who'd been riding a bicycle near the highway. Chris was flown by helicopter to a hospital, where he woke up handcuffed to a gurney.

"The only thing on my mind was, 'Had I killed somebody?'"

Losing control of his vehicle, Chris "launched [it] over a guardrail," and rolled it. The victim had a broken pelvis and was undergoing surgery. Chris suffered head injuries and broken ribs.

"I thought I had hit my bottom. Little did I know, I still had much further to go."

Chris's life was undeniably out of control. Ill-equipped to deal with life on life's terms, he acted on the assumption that his only option was to check out of reality. By this time, he was a slave to drugs and alcohol. But somehow, a seed of hope poked through the soil.

"I decided to try something new. I asked for help."

So, Chris made his first trip to rehab. However, his motives were misguided. In large part, he went to appease the courts.

"While I was in treatment, I learned my incident with the armed gunman never even made it to court. The assault charges were being dropped due to self-defense. One down, one to go. So, at the recommendations of my counselors, I agreed to attend a three-month aftercare program, which was basically a sober living house with counselors on staff."

Chris found a job and began attending 12 Step recovery meetings while awaiting sentencing for the crash he caused.

"I fell into a steady routine of work and recovery and slowly began to enjoy life again. I had been clean for about four months when I received a call from my attorney. I was indicted for my accident. I was being charged with Aggravated Assault with a Deadly Weapon, Resulting in Serious Bodily Injury. When it was all said and done, the judge showed leniency since I had completed treatment, and I was sentenced to nine months in prison with a six-year probation tail. The charge was reduced to Intoxication Vehicular Assault.

"After prison, I was released to a halfway house for three months. I now had nearly eighteen months of sobriety—but most of that was due to incarceration. I guess a better way to put it is—I was simply dry. And since I was not working a program, it was only a matter of time.

"I made it about six months before I got the bright idea to start selling pills again. I made it about another three months before I was using again. I had a pain management doctor and was once again popping Vicodin like candy. One day, I was driving after using a combo of painkillers and muscle relaxers—I was involved in another accident. It was just a fender bender, but it was bad enough for the cops to show up, and I got arrested for Driving Under the Influence. So here I am, once again on a six-year probation sentence for Intoxication Assault, in which I almost killed a man. And now, I had violated probation by receiving a DUI, in which there was another car accident. Texas was out to hang me. The first time I went to court they offered me twenty years. I spent six months in county jail fighting the case."

Chris used his time wisely—in the law library studying case law and filing appeals.

"I just wasn't willing to go away to prison for the rest of my life. Eventually, my attorney got the DA down to a five-year sentence and I signed. I was sentenced to the Texas Department of Corrections for a total of five years of incarceration. My life as I knew it was officially over."

"What about the 'three strikes and you're out' rule?" I ask.

"My first felony didn't count because I got a deferred sentence. Otherwise, I would have gotten the paragraph."

"What's 'the paragraph'?"

"It's a penal code where you're sentenced to life after three felonies."

Here, Chris explains life in Texas prisons, which are self-sufficient. Prisoners work on independent farms and inside on-site slaughterhouses. In addition, they have jobs in the library, commissary, and offices, giving them full access to confidential records.

"Yeah, the prisoners run the prisons," he tells me.

This is a universal concept I would hear from each man I interviewed, regardless of the state. I learned that while not all prisons are completely self-sufficient, most allow appointed offenders to work in capacities where they may view others' records—a practice proven unwise and even dangerous.

Chris had stints of time in jails throughout his criminal career. He did three years straight in medium and maximum-security prisons, followed by two years of probation.

> "In Texas, if you're sentenced to prison for an aggravated offense, you spend the first six months in Administrative Segregation. This means you're in a single six-by-nine cell all by yourself for twenty-three hours a day. They let you out one hour a day to shower and to make phone calls, then it's back to your cell. I'll tell ya, if you don't have a Higher Power, you find one real quick in the segregation unit of a prison cell."

Chris shares that when he was first let out of solitary confinement, he sort of missed it. He likens it to a dog feeling safe inside its kennel. But that soon dissipated, and he wanted never to go back to being locked up by himself.

"Tell me about your first day in the yard."

> "Well, I was transferred several times to many different prison units during my incarceration. Eight, to be exact. Each yard had a different vibe. Every time I'd get comfortable on a new yard and begin to make friends, I'd suddenly be transferred to a

different facility. This always happened without notice. I'd be dead asleep in the middle of the night when they'd come get me and throw me on a bus. They never told me where I was going either. Sometimes it would be thirty minutes away, sometimes it was an eight-hour bus ride, handcuffed to some of the hardest walks of life."

"Describe your first introduction to the general population."

Chris validates my understanding of initiation. "They prospect you. That's what they call it. They asked if I ran with anyone. 'No, man. I'm solo,' I said. But I ended up with the Peckerwoods. They weren't a gang—they were a bunch of white guys that looked out for each other. They weren't racist, but they were all white. Some of them had tattoos of Woody the Woodpecker."

"Were there membership dues or fees for protection?"

"Nah, but they did do a heart check. Do you know what that is?"

I shake my head and ask him to explain.

"A heart check is when two guys beat you up with your hands behind your back for thirty seconds. They only take body shots. There can't be any face marks. You'd get in trouble with the guards for fighting if they could tell."

"I heard prisons used to be very segregated back in the day. Are they still?"

Chris takes a drag off his vape pen. "Very... Yeah, the COs watched the gangs in the chow hall. We all sat at different tables. We used to call it the 'BMW'. You had the blacks, the Mexicans, and the whites.

"I'll tell ya something funny. I distinctly remember this. There was a big sign hanging in the chow hall that read something to the effect that, 'Pseudosaccharin causes cancer in lab animals.' Isn't that funny? All these guys are sitting around drinking Kool-Aid under this sign. Gives a whole other meaning to, 'Drinking the Kool-Aid,' doesn't it?"

"I guess they have nothing to lose, so why not?"

"Yeah, that's right." He takes another drag.

"I know you had to do whatever was necessary to survive, but is there anything you regret doing while you were in prison?"

Sadly, I'm not surprised when he tells me. "Yeah, I had to beat up my best friend. He got a 'D.' You know what that is? 'D'— for discipline. He left out a tattoo gun. When they found it, they did a shakedown. They searched everybody's lockers and of course, a lot of guys had contraband in their possession, so they were mad. I had to beat up my best friend and make it look good because everybody was watching. I think he ended up with some broken ribs and other stuff. But if I hadn't done that, somebody else would have taken care of it. Yeah, that's the only thing I feel bad about."

"I know getting tattoos in prison is easy, and there are many ways of doing it. How was it done while you were there?"

"Guys would pop sockets to cause a controlled fire. They would burn hair grease they purchased off commissary inside a locker, scrape the soot and combine it with water to make the ink. Guys would steal the mechanisms from 'exit' signs and make rotary tattoo guns by combining the guts of the 'exit' signs with needles stolen from the infirmary."

Ingenious. I'll learn many different ways of building tattoo guns and making ink as my project progresses.

"What about accomplishments? Did you do anything with your time that you're proud of?"

"I tutored guys so they could get their GED."

In most of what follows, Chris tells his story much better than I can—with original writing taken from the document he emailed to me. A few clarifying comments and questions are marked and embedded. Only minor edits were made to his writing:

"After I'd served half of my sentence, I was released on parole. This was without a doubt the best day of my life. I still remember catching the bus to Huntsville and walking the mile past all the death row inmates on my way out the gates to

49

freedom. Words cannot describe that feeling. Without a doubt, better than any high I'd ever had. Unfortunately, that feeling wouldn't last long.

"With my newfound freedom, I found purpose once again. All the time spent locked up had fueled my hunger for a new life. I spent the first ninety days on house arrest. After that, I decided to enroll in college. My grandfather was on the board of a university. Of course, I had some hoops to jump through. I mean, it was a private, Christian institution and I was a convicted felon. Eventually, I was able to convince them to let me in and my collegiate years began.

"I had gone from a prison cell to my own apartment right on campus. Granted I was twenty-eight years old, but nonetheless, I was living the dream. I decided to major in Business Management, and in my first year, I excelled. It appeared I was finally ready for school, and thus, life. My first year outta prison, I didn't even think about using. I was still riding that pink cloud of freedom. And then came my second year…

"I had about a year and a half left on parole when one day I got the bright idea to smoke weed. It wasn't long before I fell into my old ways and began selling the stuff. I viewed myself as that cool older guy on campus with all the drug connects. Pretty soon my ego got the best of me and once again I thought I was hot shit. I had just got my license back and already I threw [on] the big rims and loud stereo in my car. Oh yeah, and can't forget about the TV screens. Everybody needs multiple TV screens in their car while they are driving. Whatever. I was a total idiot, but at the time I thought I was something else. Weed turned to pills, pills turned to coke, and once again meth. This is around the time I started using intravenously. About this time is when I also learned about the Darknet."

"What is the 'Darknet'?"

"The Darknet, or Darkweb, is an underground black market on the Internet used for buying/selling illegal goods, drugs, and services.

"Before long I was having any drug I ever wanted delivered right to my front porch. But eventually, the cops were on to me again. I had undercover agents in unmarked cars watching my house and I was getting pulled over weekly for random vehicle searches. My junior year I got pulled over making a run to pick up dope. I had in my possession several pills—which I did, in fact, have prescriptions for—but since they were not in their proper container, I got arrested for Felony Drug Possession. I did eventually beat the case, but since I was on parole at the time, it was a blatant violation. I was sent back to prison to complete the remaining three months I had left on parole. I got out and immediately started shooting up again. I was able to go back to school, but they did place me on administrative probation.

"One night I was busy studying for a final when I decided to take some Xanax. I followed that by some nasal spray Fentanyl. Little did I know I was flirting with death. For the life of me, I don't know why, but I decided I wanted to get some ice cream. This move saved my life. I drove down to the local 7-11 and next thing I knew I came to, in the back of an ambulance. That night, there just so happened to be paramedics getting gas at the same gas station. As soon as I put my car in park, I fell out and became unresponsive. The paramedic walking in to pay for his gas noticed me slumped over the wheel and revived me with Narcan. When I came to—in the back of the ambulance—all I remember was vomiting profusely, grabbing a bedpan, and shittin' my guts out. Within thirty minutes, they had revived me, and I was stable. I signed myself out of the hospital, went home, and got high. I was one-hundred percent powerless to the stuff. I was a junkie. I was an addict, and I was hopeless.

"Somehow, I made it through my junior year of college. I was officially off of parole, off probation, and had no one holding me accountable. At this point in time, I was doing whatever drug I could get my hands on. One night after a bad ketamine trip, I called up my mom. I told her about my drug use and told her I needed help. Her and my stepdad found a local treatment center, and once again I was on my way. The strange thing is, looking back I'm certain I still wasn't ready to quit. I just knew that what I was doing wasn't working, and I thought a little vacation from it all might be the answer.

"I was reintroduced to 12 Step recovery. I completed the program and was out about one month before I relapsed. The whole time I was in treatment, all I could think about was that prescription refill I had waiting at Walgreens for a hundred and fifty Norcos [Vicodin]. Of course, I began to lie to myself and say I was just going to sell them... And of course, it wasn't long before I was taking them. Within days I was again shooting meth, and ordering Fentanyl and Xanax off the Darknet.

"My senior year started off bad. I had signed up to study abroad in Australia for a semester but would soon be uninvited by the school. One morning prior to class, I drank about a half-pint of codeine cough syrup and was awakened by campus police knocking on my car window. Of course, the cop knew me, and he gave me a ride back to my apartment. He gave me some talk about buckling down and getting my life together so I could graduate. I wasn't hearing it. I went home and immediately began snorting coke so I could wake up. When that didn't work, I turned to the needle. I was a total junky and felt more alone than I did in that prison cell.

"After a few days, I again called my mom and came clean. Neither she nor I knew what to do. Her and my stepdad agreed to pick me up. I had nowhere to go, so they were going to let me stay with them. The terms were that I would get sober, find a job, and get active again in my recovery. We stopped at a hotel along the way. They didn't trust me with my own room, so we shared a room. While they were asleep, I snuck into the bathroom and railed some meth. It was all I knew how to do.

"Eventually, we did make it to their house, and soon I found work as a subcontractor. I worked every day, and every night I went to a local meeting. This time, I kept my word. I got a sponsor finally and began working The Steps. Slowly but surely my life began to change. I had about six months clean and had just completed my fifth Step with a sponsor. Then one day it hit me. I hadn't thought about using in a long time. The obsession to use had been taken from me, and at last, the miracle had happened. I was on cloud nine.

"My sponsor and I began to take meetings to a treatment center once a week. Before long I had a year clean and had worked all Twelve Steps. I even began sponsoring a few guys that had just gotten outta treatment. I would often drive over to the nearby sober living house and pick guys up to go to meetings. This was one of the happiest times in my life. I was sponsoring guys and I was living The Steps. Shit got good, and the promises began coming true in my life.[7]

---

[7] This is a reference to what AA members refer to as, "The Promises." which can be found in the Big Book on pages 83-84 of the 4th edition.

"Eventually, I got a job offer downtown and began once again chasing money. Around this time, I received the news that my grandad had passed away. Shortly after that, my dad died. He had been fighting cancer and addiction for years and had finally lost the battle. When my grandfather passed, he left all of his business to his grandkids. Shortly after that, I sold my share for a large sum. I used the money to buy a new truck, a Harley, and to furnish my new house downtown.

"I began my career as a heavy equipment operator. Before I knew it, I was working sixty hours a week and had quit going to meetings. After all, I was cured... Yeah right. I guess I missed that whole part about, 'All we have is a daily reprieve contingent upon spiritual conditioning.'[8] It was about three months after I quit going to meetings before I relapsed yet again. Once again, I was ordering drugs off the Darknet and back at it. I eventually did manage to pull myself out of it for a brief stint and once again got dry.

"Then, in the spring I was snowboarding and had a bad spill. I hit a giant patch of ice, lost control, and went tumbling. I woke up on a Fentanyl drip. I was told I had shattered my femur and pelvis. It took me three months before I learned to walk again. They had put a rod, plate, two screws, and two nails in the left

---

[8] This is a quote from the Big Book on page 85 of the 4th edition.

side of my body. But more importantly, they had put Fentanyl in my body. Opiates had me in a chokehold. I was once again a slave to them. I would spend the next three years fighting a losing battle. Again, I was floating from job to job and using daily.

"In 2017, probably the worst thing that could happen to an addict like me happened. I won thirty-thousand dollars through an online sports gambling website. I had also just received my annual earnings through our family's business. During this time, I was spending about fifteen-hundred dollars a week ordering Fentanyl through the Darknet. I lived every day in a state of total numbness.

"Around this time, I began dating a stripper and we blew money faster than it came in. I bought her a Cadillac and paid for us to fly out to Hawaii for two weeks where I lived in a total state of oblivion. On the flight there, I was so messed up everyone just assumed I was handicapped, and she was my caregiver—which in hindsight was actually pretty spot on. They had to wheel me off the airplane in a wheelchair for Christ's sake—which I was told I soon fell out of. I vaguely remember Hawaii. I smuggled Fentanyl onto the airplane in nasal spray containers and used it all day every day during our stay. Upon our return home, she left. The money was gone, and thus was she.

"I began renting a basement downtown from some guy and I continued my job as a heavy equipment operator. Then one night it happened again. I had ordered some Fentanyl powder from the Darknet and decided this time instead of diluting it in solution for nasal spray, I would just snort the powder straight instead. Again, I woke up in the back of an ambulance puking my guts out as the result of Narcan. I had overdosed yet again. I knew I needed help but didn't know how to seek it. My family had written me off, and I absolutely couldn't get clean on my own. The withdrawals were too much to bear.

"I eventually pulled myself together enough to save for a deposit on a house. I got a new job as an equipment operator and although I was using, it had the appearance of being in control. It wasn't long before I fell even further, though. I was so sick and miserable, and you know what they say, 'Misery loves company.' I basically began dumpster diving for companionship. If you had dope, you always had a place to stay at my house.

"I met a cute girl who always seemed to have a large amount of methamphetamine around. She moved in and it wasn't long before I realized she had ties to a cartel. She began running stolen cars outta my garage and selling large amounts of crystal meth and heroin outta my house. Throughout this whole time, I had always somehow managed to avoid the drug that had taken my brother's life, but it wasn't long before I, too, began using heroin.

"My new place transformed into a trap house almost overnight. It didn't take long for me to realize I was under surveillance. One day, I left my house to go pick up some heroin. I had just purchased a half ounce and was pulled over by police. I didn't know what to do. I knew I was gonna go away to jail for a long time and was terrified of the withdrawals I would face. So, I made a deal. I agreed to be a CI [Cooperative Informant] for the DEA. If I agreed to give the names of my suppliers, they would drop all charges. So, I did… Well, not to rat out my dealer, that would almost definitely be a death sentence. No, I simply said that I would in order for them to release me. So, it was arranged.

"Agent Gary and I began meeting weekly to discuss any intel I had obtained. I just kept bullshitting him though. This went on for about a month. Then one morning before work, I stopped to re-up at my supplier's house. When I got to work, I was told we weren't working that day due to a large amount of our equipment being 'downed'. So, I snorted some Fentanyl and left the job site. Before long, I was too messed up to drive and pulled over at 7-11 to rest. I woke up and my Jeep was surrounded by DEA and the city task force with guns drawn. I was arrested and charged with my third DUI. I also had in my possession—a large amount of meth, heroin, Fentanyl, Xanax,

Oxys, scales, baggies, and syringes. I was held without bail on ten charges, including Felony Drug Trafficking and Manufacturing. My life was over… once again.

"When you're in jail there's really not much to do. In the past, I had always used this time to pray and negotiate plea bargains with my Higher Power… 'God, if you just let them drop these charges, I promise I'll never use again… God, if you just allow that judge to show leniency, I promise I'll get my shit together.' The funny thing is that prior to being arrested this time, I had actually begun to pray to GOD once again. I mean, I knew my life was completely outta control, and I knew I had to stop using drugs… I just didn't know how exactly to go about getting help.

"In those weeks prior to being locked up, I spent a lot of time working step zero. You know, that's the step when you're still using like a banshee, but you are actually *thinking* about getting sober. God, I spent a lot of time on step zero. I knew I needed it, I just didn't know how to go about it. As I mentioned, the withdrawals were too much for me to bear. I believe me being arrested was actually GOD answering my prayers for sobriety… or at least it was his way of preserving my life a lil' bit longer.

"Anyway, I spent four months in county jail fighting the case. The DEA was no longer on my side since I hadn't even given them one single viable lead, much less a name. That's why I believe they stacked the charges on me. I think they were hoping I would crack under the pressure and at least give them a name. It didn't work though. Honestly, I felt safe in jail. I was no longer living with sketchy people who I'm sure were out looking for me, plus I didn't have any drugs to abuse. This thought was reinforced by my mother. Every time I went to jail, she would always tell me on the phone that she slept better when I was locked up. There's a sobering thought for you. But it's true. I was simply a liability to myself.

"Eventually, my public defender did do some astonishing work in my favor though. She told me that while I was incarcerated, the state had just signed a new bill making possession of any controlled substance now just a misdemeanor. Unfortunately for me, I did have those scales and baggies on me though. So, after about five months in jail, I finally reached a deal with the DA. If I would plead to one charge on manufacturing codeine, all the other felonies would disappear. The day I signed I received one hundred days 'time served' for DUI number three, but for the Manufacturing charge I would have to complete six months of work release, followed by two years of probation. It was a sweetheart of a deal, to say the least.

"So, in the winter of 2019 I was released from work release. And guess what I did? That's right, I started shooting up again. While at work release, I had met some new connects and it was too easy not to say yes. During my time there I had managed to save up a few hundred dollars and with this, I purchased a van. So, when I was released, I was living in that van, with my dog in the Walmart parking lot... because that's what we do as tweakers, we go to Walmart. Anyway, you would think after all I had been through that this time I'd get it, right? Well, I hadn't. You see, that's what we do as addicts—we use. And without any form of treatment or 12 Step recovery, I was still suffering from untreated alcoholism and addiction. I use the two [words] interchangeably. You see alcoholism is addiction, and addiction is alcoholism. I mean, pick your poison. The only difference is alcohol is legal and can be purchased at the corner store. I've often said the only difference between my dealer and my doctor was that one of them accepts Medicaid. Anyway, so I managed to make it outta jail a whole forty-eight hours before I found myself back in treatment. How exactly this happened is a story in and of itself."

Some of us believe the brain of an addict/alcoholic is wired differently than that of "normal" people. Our basic physiological processes differ, thus causing the inability to stop by willpower alone—no matter how desperately we want to.

Chris continues...

"The night after being released, I was in my van in that Walmart parking lot. I had gone into the pharmacy and purchased a box of a hundred syringes. When I got out to my van, I decided to load up as much dope as I could possibly fit inside the plunger. I remember registering.[9] And before I did the shot, I thought to myself, 'It would be pretty nice if I just didn't wake up tomorrow.' Well, I did wake up. 'Shit.' I was a failure at living and a failure at dying. I didn't realize it at the time, but that was the gift of desperation I so desperately needed. I knew I absolutely could not keep living like I was— using. But I also knew, I absolutely could not keep living without using. What was I to do?

"That morning I began driving around the city. I had no idea where I was going, I just kept driving in circles. Before I knew it a force unbeknownst to me had taken the wheel, and I found myself entering onto the highway, headed towards my parents' house. When I arrived, the sun had gone down. I noticed they were doing construction on their front porch. So, I crept my way down the set of outside stairs through the darkness, and to their back porch. When I got to the back sliding glass door, I noticed an index card taped to the window. It read, 'In case of an emergency, call...' and it had my mom and my stepdad's cell phone numbers listed. I knocked on the door and within seconds my mom and stepdad appeared with obvious worry on their faces. My mom opened the doors and hugged me. She told me she had put that note on the door because the night before she had had a premonition.

---

[9] In intravenous drug use, "registering" means to draw back the plunger until blood can be seen inside the syringe, indicating the needle has hit a vein.

"Evidently, this feeling of doom had come over her. She had this overwhelming sensation that I had died from a drug overdose. She had placed the note on the door just in case the police had to come to the house to inform her that I was dead. She worried that since the construction was taking place on their front porch that law enforcement might not be able to reach her. After all, she was familiar with the formalities—being that she had already been awakened once before in the middle of the night by cops telling her one son had died. I mean how crazy is that?! The very night I loaded up a giant shot of dope and said a silent prayer not to wake up, my mom gets a sudden feeling of fear—an intuition that I had died from a drug overdose. I began to break down. I mean, a total breakdown. Like tears flowing, snot slingin', total breakdown. I was holding my mom in my arms, crying and then I said it. 'Mom, I need help… I'd like to go back into treatment.'

"So, the arrangements were made, and the miracle workers at rehab did their thing. That very next day I was sitting in detox thanking God for bringing me to this point. Sure, I'd been here before, but this time it was different. I had received that gift of desperation, and I knew in my heart I was willing to go to any length to get this thing. I simply had to have recovery at all costs. I needed it just like I needed the air in my lungs. I was gonna get this thing, and I was gonna make it work. If my counselors wanted me to do a headstand in a bucket of shit, my motto was, 'Bring on the turds!' My time in rehab was magical.

I met some of the best friends I'd ever had. I shared some of the best laughs and cries I'd ever had. I was finally exactly where I needed to be.

"It was suggested when I got out that I attend ninety meetings in ninety days. So, I did exactly that. It was suggested that I get a sponsor, work The Steps, and pick up a service commitment. So I did just that. Whatever they suggested, I was gonna do. After all, I fuckin' sucked at running my own life. Hell, if I'm driving the bus, we're all going off the cliff. So, I began working the steps, and shit got good—quick. In no time I went from being homeless to actually becoming a homeowner. I went from living in and driving a van (illegally, I might add), to possessing a driver's license with full coverage insurance on a new car. Granted I had to get one of those nifty blow-n-go devices in it, but dammit, I was legit! The treatment center has always had a special place in my heart. I had experienced recovery here before, and now here I am experiencing it again. This time, I've gone through the program and I'm an alumnus. It means something special to me to be a part of that.

"I decided that perhaps one day, my story might be able to benefit others. One of the principles I learned early on, is that one addict/alcoholic helping another is without parallel. So, I decided that maybe all the time I had spent drinking and drugging could actually serve to benefit me professionally. I began pursuing my CAC [Certified Addiction Counselor] certification and sharing my story whenever I got the chance.

"I think COVID kinda came as a shock to all of us. It completely disrupted life as we know it. But then again, isn't that exactly what addiction and alcoholism does? I mean, it gets to a certain point, and then it is a total disruption of life as we know it. So, it's my firm belief that if anyone is equipped to make it through times like these, it's us addicts and alcoholics in the world.

"When I came to rehab, I was asked about my coping skills. What have I done in the past to cope? The honest answer was I didn't have any. All I ever did was use. If things were bad, I used. If things were good, I used. I used every day of the week that ended in Y, and twice on Sundays. This was all I ever knew…"

"What do you do to cope with feelings in healthy ways today?" I ask Chris.

"I have a therapist I see, go to meetings, be of service—I have sponsees I work with—talk to my sponsor, pray and meditate."

In his writing, Chris goes on:

"… So naturally, I had to ask for help. After all, I had no idea how to live sober. I mean, sure I had brief stints of sobriety in the past, but nothing that ever seemed to last. So today I eat, breathe, sleep, and live recovery. I learned that saying, 'Yes,' to my recovery is the best contingency plan I could come up with. So naturally, whenever I'm asked to share my story I say, 'Yes.' I'd be a liar if I told you, it has all been rainbows and kittens along the way, though.

"Just four months ago, I was out at the local skatepark trying to relive some of my glory days as a youth when I had a gnarly spill. I fell off my skateboard and totally blew out my wrist. I shattered it with multiple displacement fractures through the bone, joint, and cartilage. It happened on a Thursday, and Friday morning I found myself in an oh too familiar place— under the knife. I had surgery on my wrist, and it took a plate and eleven screws to put my wrist back together. Only this time, I was prepared. As soon as I went into the ER, I told the hospital staff that I was an addict in recovery and that they probably would be better off not feeding me any narcotics. After my surgery, I was asked if I was certain I didn't want any oxy. I told them, 'Of course I do. I want all of them… and that's the problem. One is too many and a thousand is never enough.'

"There's no stopping this train once it gets going. I've learned from my past that if I take anything whatsoever to alter my state of mind, that's no good. That was exactly my problem. I always considered myself to have a very low tolerance for reality and the bullshit people that it consisted of. So, I always needed something to alter my perception. And like I said, I just always used. If I was feeling, I used so I wouldn't have to feel… If I was numb, I used so that I could feel. There was no escaping it. Today, I have found that I no longer have that need to escape.

"Recovery has taught me the true meaning of friendship and what it feels like to care for someone else besides myself. And that's honestly why I am here. That's why I'm working at a treatment center today, and that's why I'm sharing my story with you. I'm not really a huge fan of speaking in front of people… But honestly, there's no place I'd rather be than in a room full of fellow addicts and alcoholics. This is my tribe. You are my people. In these rooms, I find that I can simply be myself and that that's good enough. There's no judgment within these walls. We've all had our brushes with death, and I believe we are all miracles.

"If you are struggling with a Higher Power or need proof of some type of God, just look around. The fact that some of us are still breathing is all the proof I need. I know how to count my blessings today, and it starts with the fact that I'm on the green side of the dirt and have a pulse. But this experience right here also has been a blessing for me, and I want y'all to know that.

"Thank you for allowing me to be here today and for hearing my story. I hope that if nothing else, you at least can find hope in what I've shared. Because I assure you, if an addict like me can find recovery, then so can you. Remember that, and never lose hope. Sometimes it's all we have... but sometimes that's all we need."

ROPING TO REDEMPTION

"My quickest release was to go for the bottle. That was the best way to deal with things. And it was trusty. It was there. And it was like, my best friend. My worst enemy."

Is it the massive amount of caffeine he's ingested, or the nagging urge to smoke? Brad clips along at a quick pace. While he's heartfelt and thorough in telling me his story, he speaks so fast that later transcription will be a monumental feat. He gulps his Monster energy drink as we talk, and indicates he's had several that day. Right away, it's clear—Brad is a man on the move.

As an Owner, Human Resource Contact, Marketing Coordinator, and Customer Service Agent, Brad is left with limited spare time. Surely these demands of his start-up business are exhausting, but he manages them well. So, I'm grateful when he takes a Sunday evening to sit down with me for a Zoom teleconference.

At precisely five o'clock, his face appears on my screen. He's bent over, intently staring at what I presume is the bottom of a laptop. With an outstretched arm, he looks as if he's tuning a radio or something. Then, he stands back to evaluate the signal strength of his Internet connection. Finally satisfied, he turns away and maneuvers something behind him.

"I'm gonna pull up a chair a little closer," he says.

Curious, I survey his surroundings. "Looks like you have some sort of aquaponics happenin' there."

"Yeah... That was like... a project that I've been working on since I got out." He plops into the lawn chair.

"Gotcha... So basically, like I said—I want to do, like, a speaker meeting."

"OK."

"And if you don't mind, I'll just let you tell your story and kinda interject with my questions."

"OK."

I don't want to waste Brad's time with small talk, so I jump right in. "I'd like to start with your upbringing and what your family life was like."

"Yeah, I don't think we're getting that great of a connection. I just kinda lost you for a second."

"Shit!" The last thing I want is for technical difficulties to derail our interview.

"Yeah... I was hoping that we would, just because I'd be able to smoke cigarettes out here. You know? That's the addict in me... I'll just run into the house and reconnect, kick back and go from there. Will that work?"

"Ok, that sounds good."

"Alright, I'll reconnect in two minutes."

I had asked Mike—an oldtimer and mutual friend, whom I respect a great deal—if he knew of anyone who might be interested in contributing to this book. I told him about my idea, stressing my mission. I was looking for men who had overcome tremendous odds to gain recovery, who had done hard time for alcohol or drug-related crime, and who now want to give back by carrying the message. Mike contacted Brad on my behalf. There were several calls, texts, and emails in setting up our meeting. With each exchange, Brad was polite and professional. Later he would prove to be patient, tolerant, and articulate.

> Exactly two minutes pass. Then Brad reappears. "Yeah… See the router's here in the house. The greenhouse is like, thirty feet away, but the signal strength… Oh well, this is what we get."
> He takes another swig of his Monster.

"Well, I'm glad you're a trooper…" Later, I would notice this unintentional pun. "So did you hear my speech before we cut out?"

"Yeah, basically just speaker meeting kind of stuff."

"Yeah—so I'm all ears whenever you're ready."

"OK… I was born on a military base in Germany, then [we] came back home. My father was in the United States military.

My mom was from here, as well. They were married and everything."

"Did your family move around a lot?"

"No, my dad did one enlistment and that was it. Then he was a truck driver after that, so he was always gone. I don't remember a whole lot of him—at all. My parents divorced when I was like, three or four. And I was kind of raised between my uncle, my grandparents, and my mom. My mom was kind of a party girl and stuff like that."

"Was she an alcoholic?"

"I don't know. I can't judge anyone an alcoholic other than myself, really. Some people in my family can reign it in. And I can't…

"This is really a rural area. Everybody kind of knows everybody and whose parents were who and it's just kind of… It's kind of cool to come back to, but… I mean, it's just the way it is here, so…

"I was raised as a normal kind of Mormon kid. I played sports and never really drank a whole lot. But when I did the first time, I was a blackout drunk and I was like, probably fourteen."

"What happened?"

"My mom had shacked up with a farmer and they had a bar in the house and everything else. And one night I just got a bottle of whiskey to see what it would do. It tasted like shit, and I about puked. Then, about thirty minutes later, I was like, 'This makes me feel good.' Yeah, you know? I just [drank] more and more and then just kind of... 'Wow...'

"So, like, right off the bat—alcoholic and blackout drinker. 'Cause I woke up the next morning in my underwear, on the living room floor with a sleeping bag over me. And then tried to play that off. 'I didn't do nothin'.' I puked up cheap whiskey all over the house. But you know, that's my first real experience with it. And then it was off to my grandparents. And then, there wasn't a whole lot of that. Maybe a beer here and there.

"So, then I joined the Army right out of high school. And being in the military and doin' what I did—it's just a given. I wanted to be an Army Ranger. Went through basic training, AIT [Advanced Individual Training], Jump School, then into RIP and everything else."[10]

"What's RIP?"

"Ranger Indoctrination Program.[11] So, Ranger regiment is actually kind of considered special operations. It's level one

---

[10] "Jump School" is The United States Army Airborne School, which oversees introductory paratrooper training.
[11] Ranger Indoctrination Program (RIP) is an intense, eight-week course intended to assess a soldier's fortitude under extreme conditions.

special operations. So, it's all the training that you need to go through before you even get to a Ranger battalion. And then once you're there, everybody's drunk and brawlin'. It's a very spartan-type life. Very spartan. It was just kind of one of those accepted things.

"I did really well in the military. Got promoted fast. Graduated Ranger School in like, two years. And then right after that, sniper school. I was a sniper squad leader and a sniper team leader. And then I got orders to go to Korea. I went to Korea for a year. And that's like, when my first drinking—getting myself in trouble over it—kind of started. And I got reprimanded. It was an incident on New Year's Eve, and we'd all been drinking. And it was just one of those kinds of things that happened in an infantry battalion in Korea."

"Will you share what happened?"

"There were several incidents. It wasn't just one. It was like, one of those things where I kept gettin' away with shit because I was this kind of badass soldier guy. But that just kind of like, instilled in me—looking back now—a sense of entitlement because I kept getting away with a lot.

"The big incident was... It was New Year's Eve. Basically, I'd gotten drunk. I mean, everybody had gotten drunk. Some of the guys in my squad, my junior soldiers—they got in a fight. The company commander basically wanted to call the military police in and have the MPs take care of all this stuff. And they came and got me. It's New Year's Eve. I'm obviously shit faced. And my company commander wants to see me because my soldiers beat the fuck out of each other. I try and tell him we're gonna try to take care of this in house—not get the military police involved. He said somethin' to me, and I just lost it. I went off on him. I let him have it. And I was kind of in a blackout. I don't remember a whole lot of it. My friends just kind of drug me back down to my room. It was bad.

The company commander wanted to really hit me hard with, like, an article fifteen, which is a non-judicial punishment. But my platoon leader actually kind of talked him out of it and put me in for a rehabilitative transfer to a different company. Yeah, that was when I told the company commander, he was a fucking idiot. But you know, Korea is like, one of those places in the military where there's a lot of drinking going on. And that was like, my first time I really got into trouble with it.

"So, after I finished up that year in Korea, I was offered kind of a choice of assignments. I actually went to Fifth Ranger Training Battalion, which is the mountain phase of Army Ranger School. So, I was an instructor there. Basically, the drinking stuff progressed. Got a DUI, and the DUI was enough to kind of alert the commander that, 'This guy has a problem,' because of what happened in Korea.

"I actually got two DUIs. I got arrested for two DUIs. I never got convicted of those two DUIs. Again, because of me being in the military. A lot of the local Sheriffs are ex-Army Rangers. And that was like—my entire re-enlistment bonus went to a bribe to get out of a DUI. And then the second one, it just somehow disappeared. I don't know who did it. I don't know what happened, but the sheriff's department lost all that stuff."

"So that's more of the entitlement… feeding into that."

"Mmm-hmm. My history is starting to follow me, and this is where I'm starting to realize where my past kind of leads into things. And so basically, I was told, 'You're either going to rehab or you're just gonna get kicked out of the Army.' So, I went to rehab. That was like my first experience with AA.

My first meeting was where I went to a military treatment facility, and we were required to go to AA meetings every night after we did our treatment stuff. The first meeting I went to was, like, in the hood—like, ghetto. And I'm a farm kid. We get there and there's only, like— Everybody was black. The only white people in there were me and this other girl that was in rehab with me. We were just kind of shocked. You know? But as the meeting progressed, you'd listen to speakers and stuff like this. Something just clicked. It was just, like, 'This is foreign, but it's still where I need to be.' So, after that meeting, it just, it kind of just clicked and I wanted it."

"Did you stay sober after that introduction to the program?"

"So, I went through treatment. Went back to my unit. I was sober for about a year or so. Relapsed. Got a DUI. So now, at this point, they're basically… My security clearance is gone. My military career is pretty much over. One of our camp PAs [Physician's Assistant] was a special forces medic, and he basically came to me and said, 'I could just get you a medical discharge, if that's the route that you want to do.' And I accepted. So, I just took a medical… It was an honorable discharge, but for me to stay in the military at the time—I just didn't see it.

"I got out and started working for a tree company—cutting trees, climbing trees. And the ropes experience from like, the repelling and the mountaineering, just kind of transferred over into climbing trees. And I got a job doing that. I just kinda got hooked on climbing trees with a chainsaw for whatever reason. At first, it was like, 'Oh, wow!' You know? And I was looking for ego boost-type shit when I was young like that. And so, it just stuck. And so, we were doing that. I was right outta the military… I was a shithead. You know when I look back, I'm just like, 'Damn. I was a little fucking shit.' But I kind of got fired from one job."

"Why did you get fired?"

"It was, like, I got fired, but it was just one of those, 'Fuck you, I don't really care,' kind of things. I got terminated, but I also kind of said, 'Screw it! This really kind of sucks.' And there was a lot of political stuff goin' on with that, too. And at the time, when I was younger like that, the way I dealt with social interactions with people who weren't of my military brotherhood… You know what I mean? I was very abrupt and rude with people. And just short. I was a little asshole. So, there was a lot of ego stuff goin' on there. Entitlement and everything else.

"And you know, that was really when the drinking starts hitting the point where you like, need it every day. I just really had to have it. Before that, it was all party here and there. And you know, there's dumb incidents, like where I passed out on the golf course in a hurricane. But I don't like trying to glamorize that kind of stuff. You kind of see the progression as you really stop and take a look at your life.

"And so… made bad choices. Still drinkin'. Another brush with the law. Actually, kicked somebody out of my house at gunpoint, which you're not allowed to do. That's against the law… But I'm still a young Army Ranger. More brushes with the law—little misdemeanor type stuff."

"What type of misdemeanor stuff?"

"DUIs, Driving Under Restraint… is basically… is mostly traffic—moving violations. I was without a driver's license for ten years—that sucked. Just continuing drinking whenever I could. I just didn't wanna be sober, pretty much. It's not that I wanted to be drunk. It's just that I didn't wanna be sober. You know? And I was just learning how to deal with that more and more with a bottle. So, I got in trouble with that."

"Why do you think you needed alcohol to cope? Was it because of your military experience, or you didn't learn healthy ways to do that when you were younger?"

"I think it's all of the above. I think in most cases, with me anyway, it's not one specific thing. It's a combination of several different things. You can't say it's all the military, the PTSD, and this and that. Or, you can't say, 'I was abused as a child,' or this and that. You know? It's a combination of everything. And the reason I did it—it was comfort. It was escape. It was relief from anxiety, and stress, and fear, and shame, and guilt. And all that stuff that we drink and use over. Everything is interwoven. So, it's not necessarily one cause.

"It's kind of like, when I talk to people about their trees—trying to explain to 'em why their tree is dying. It's not the aphids, and it's not the compaction of the soil. And it's not the over-pruning. It's a combination of everything. Drought. And when all these factors are met, then the tree is just overwhelmed. And that's the way I kind of feel. That's the way I can best explain it. When I have all these outside factors that are kind of bombarding me, I feel a little overwhelmed. And my quickest release was to go for the bottle. That was the best way to deal with things. And it was trusty. It was there. And it was like, my best friend. My worst enemy. I can't cite one specific… you know… Why did I do what I did? It's complicated. Still, I try to unravel it in my own head…

"Came back home for a while and still continuing to drink. Didn't wanna be in that situation that I put myself in with who would later become my ex-wife. We went out to Vegas. Got married. And it was just, just bad from the get-go. And that was like, my out. I'd get home every night and into the garage and everything else.

"And so, we were together for about two years. Finally… I got another DUI. And she pretty much… kind of… basically left me in jail. Didn't bond me out. Got money from my boss that I was working for to bond me out, so I could get back to work. And she took it. It was this scandalous thing. But you know, after that, it was just straight downhill. Bad, bad, bad. Cheap motels. Just that 'gutter bravado' that they talk about in the Big Book.[12] And it just finally broke me, you know? Humility and everything else just forced me to go back and live with my parents again.

"I had a cousin that had gone through the Salvation Army program. And my aunt was like, really… not pushing it on me,

---

[12] This is a reference to a story titled, "Gutter Bravado," which can be found in the Big Book on pages 501-511 of the 4th edition.

but my family just basically said, 'You know, you need to do this, or you just need to leave, because—it's not that we don't love you—it's that we're just tired of watching you kill yourself.' So, you know, that hit… It's like, 'Fuck!' Some of the stuff I did. But you know, you don't think of it at the time. You do, but it's kinda like—brush it off. 'Cause at the time I'm just thinkin' of that next drink. You know? 'Cause when I'm drinking, all I can think of is—How can I get it? How can I get more? How long is it going to last? How am I going to cover it up? Because being in a Mormon community, everybody knows who the drunks are. I did some meetings here fifteen years ago, and a cousin of mine sponsored me back then. So, everybody's like, 'Which side of the family are you on?' You know? I'm on the drunk side, not the good Mormon side."

"Do you feel like alcoholism is something you inherited?"

"I don't know. I don't know if I buy into all that. I mean, there's all the research and stuff like that. I've talked to therapists, and they say genetics don't do it… I don't know. Maybe a genetic mental predisposition, and it's combined with a physical predisposition—as far as the allergy goes. It's above my pay grade.

"So basically, off to that Salvation Army program. And it was like a six-month program. It was really good. You know, it was. It was a lot of religion, and if you could get past that, then you had a chance. That was, like, the first time that I had the experience of being in a lot of meetings with people who were of different religions. And now they're in the Salvation Army program, which is a Christian-based community. I kind of started to understand a little bit more about the God of my understanding, and not the God that I was baptized to believe in. So that kind of opened my eyes up. It was like, a lot of meetings. Got to meet people that you become friends with. Some make it, some don't. And you know, I certainly didn't. It took me a long time to get a solid year.

'So, I landed a job in the mountains at a hotel. In the Salvation Army program, you have to work. Anyway, we had to go up to the mountains one day. And there's like a bunch of stuff from the hotel that they're donating. And I just ran into this ex-military guy, and he saw the way I was taking charge of things, and he offered me a job. Found out that I was an arborist and basically hired me on the spot. He's like, 'Come back tomorrow, we'll talk with HR, and sit down and have lunch. We have dorms here for you to move into. We're aware of your situation.' And it was just, like, one of those God moments. You know? You're just like, 'How the fuck does this happen?'

"So moved up there. Took the job and hit meetings. This whole time, I forgot to mention, I'm without a driver's license from those DUIs—from years ago—that I never took care of. But I'm up in the mountains and hittin' meetings. And that's when I ran into Mike. So, it was like, right off the bat—Mike is cool.

He got me up there, cuttin' firewood for him. Yeah, I dig Mike. He plays into the rest of my stories.

"So yeah, up there in the mountains—it was cool. Working at the hotel. So did that for a few years, and I stayed sober for a while and still ran into Mike and hit meetings. And it was kind of a revolving door thing. You know?"

"You mean going in and out of the program?"

"Yeah… And sometimes Mike needed help with firewood. He was always the first person that I'd call when my shit went south. Or when I just had an issue with something.

"But I was at the hotel, in the mountains, for two and a half years. And met a gal working—she was working there, as well. She had property, and she invited me to come over to do tree work at her house. One thing led to another and [we] pummeled into bed, and then it was just… it just turned out to be a very, very toxic relationship. It led to the police getting called. So that was domestic violence. I did stay away [from the program] for a while but continued to try and stay sober. And then finally she kind of pleaded for me to come back and, 'I need you here,' and this whole thing. And I did. And it was just that toxic, toxic relationship.

"Eventually, one night it blew up. And traditionally with her, it was like right before Christmas—and maybe it was me. Right before Christmas is when we had our issues. It was Christmas Eve one year, and Christmas Eve the next year—and I woke up in jail. Got bonded out one year, and the next year I didn't. So anyway, this time it was serious. I mean, it was an incident that scared me. Police got called, and I was kind of waiting for 'em. Which isn't a good thing, and fortunately, nothing happened and ever became of that."

"Do you want to tell me what happened?"

"It's just complicated… But, well… Not trying to deflect or anything, but she was just… She would drink and she would get combative. And I felt like I was tent-packed most of the time and I had really nowhere to escape to. You know, we lived twelve miles from town—in the mountains. And I was just tent-packed, and there was nowhere for me to go. Looking back now, I should have just got out. I should've stayed out the first time. But I came back.

"And one night, it was Christmas Eve. Something just… dumb. I came home, and I was tired, I'd been splitting wood. We were gonna watch football and do something. But she came home. I was probably passed out or taking a nap—same thing back then.

"But she started drinking. I came to. Started fighting and she basically hit me in the face with a wine bottle. And then all the combative little incidents that we'd get in before that, I was always trying to either escape… You know, there's several times I'd take my tent and [go] up into the mountains for a couple days, and then come back down. There's nowhere to escape. I got fed up with it, and when she hit me with the wine bottle it just… Honestly, it was just blind, red, homicidal rage. And I… you know… I choked her. I let her up. And I realized that split second, it's like—I either kill 'er right now or I don't. And it's just like, I'm this fucking close. I just know I can't. You know? But I was literally that close." Brad pinches his forefinger to his thumb, letting just a sliver of light pass through.

"After that, it's like, 'Ahh shit, here comes the cops. I might as well finish off anything that's left in the house.' So, the cops came and got me. And off to the county jail I went, yet again. And this time, I caught a felony. So, it was Felony Menacing. Which, you know when I look back, all this little peddly shit I think I'm getting away with is just fuckin' all going into a file with the DA at the end of the day. And it's a lot of priors that I got away with a lot of the times—most of the time. And it kind of conditioned me, that I was entitled. I could use veteran status and get leniency from the court and stuff. So, I kind of used that. And I did feel entitled."

"Does that sense of entitlement, or defiant attitude still crop up?"

"Well, yeah, it does… the defiant attitude. Like, I still have to go do this, um… In order to get off parole, I have to do this

Domestic Violence Evaluation. And all the treatment and stuff that I went in prior to gettin' thrown in prison and then while I was in prison… I was like, 'Man, I gotta do more of this stuff?'

"And my parole officer is like, 'You don't have to. But, if you wanna get off parole you do.'

"And I'm like, 'Well, shit.' I keep putting it off. And it's sittin' on the kitchen table. I looked at it this morning. I'm in the pre-contemplation phase of doing it. And I should have done it nine months ago, but it's one of those things that… I'm still defiant, and I'll do it when I'm God damn good and ready. You know?

"So anyway, off to jail again I go. And I actually bond out— Mike bonds me out. My VA disability checks started coming in. I had a bunch of back checks while I was in county jail, and he bonded me out. I got set up in a hotel for a while, and then I started working at some stables. I come from a ranching and agricultural type background. I was just fittin' in with the cowboys. I did that for a while, and then I met another gal, and thought everything was great.

"Meanwhile, I was on probation. I was on felony probation— not really taking all this stuff seriously. I was going to classes that I had to take. Just kind of poking along. Worked the whole season while I was up in the mountains and saved up money. Moved back down to the city. Started up a little tree service.

We were blissfully fucking happy, but I was on a court ordered alcohol monitor. So, I wasn't drinking. And if I was drinking, you know, the monitor would definitely go off, and I'd get in trouble and be put back in jail.

"So, I was able to stay sober for a year, wearing this monitor. And in that year, got a little tree business goin' and [we were] building a life together. She's just out of a bad relationship and we think this is all gonna be great. And then, the year on the ankle monitor—and they took it off. So, I'd already been planning what I was going to do a couple weeks ahead of time. You know? So, I went and got a six-pack and I figured, well if I get a six-pack what fuckin' good is that? Might as well get a pint to go along. So, I did. And I celebrated them cutting my frickin' ankle bracelet off by getting drunk. She wasn't happy with that.

"I woke up the next morning. She was gone. She had to go do something with the tree business. I was hungover. I'm in trouble. I'm feeling like an asshole. The way I know how to deal with things is to get another bottle. So, I went and got a bottle and another six-pack. Came home.

"The next thing I remember, we were scuffling. To this day, I don't know exactly what happened until I really came out of it, and she was biting my nose. You can still literally see the teeth marks on my nose. And then all the scratches on me… Don't know what started it, don't know who instigated it. All I know is she's on me, and she's not letting go. Had to gouge her eye to even get her to let go. And then I was just like, 'What the fuck?! Calm down. I'm on probation.' And all the sudden, it's like, 'What's going on? What's going on?' I just kind of snapped out of that blackout. I go into the bathroom. I look at my nose. I just say to her, 'Look what you did to my nose.'

"And she's like, 'Well, look what you did to my eye.' And then she goes to tackle me. And when she tackles me, we tumble into the garden tub, and she breaks a rib on the downspout. And that kind of takes the air out of her. She just kind of walks out the house, just trying to calm down, cool off… Whatever. She's covered in blood. Swollen up eye. Neighbors ask what happened.

"As soon as she walks out, I know the cops are coming. So, I'm just like, 'Well, here they come. Just finish off whatever else I got in the house and wait for them to come.

"So, I'm on the bed, passed out. I hear the bathroom window break. And then I hear an explosion, which I recognize as a flash-bang grenade. And then I smell tear gas. So, I'm in my pajamas. I'm like, they just gassed the house. 'I give up.' So, get arrested. Go to jail. Get booked in there. Eventually, I was charged with Second Degree Aggravated Assault—looking at twelve to twenty-four because it was Aggravated, and I was on felony probation. That is a— Waking up in a county jail like that, knowing that you had something going, and you just flushed it down the toilet... It's just a terrible fucking feeling."

"Do you think maybe during blackouts you went back to being in the military, and so you just started fighting with whoever was there?"

"I've heard that. Like, witnesses afterwards—they've said, 'Yeah, you were callin' names,' and this and that. 'You weren't fuckin' here.' That's kind of like... The fucked-up thing about it is... You know, sometimes you wish that there was frickin' video footage of you doin' this shit. And then sometimes you're thankful there's not.

"Anyway, Mike—he put money on the inmate's phone and stuff like that. So, he's calling me. I guess my girlfriend calls him right afterward. 'Cause, you know, she always knew that Mike was my sponsor and— Or at least a very good close-mouthed friend. And so, she called him, and you know he's like, 'Hey, this is what's going on...'

"I did nine months in county jail. I finally accepted a plea, which would have been Second Aggravated Criminal Mischief. But actually, I pled up to an F3—a Felony Three, which is more severe. But it was a nonviolent crime. So, by doing that, I was able to get an opportunity to get sentenced into the halfway house. My girlfriend—she testified. She read, like, a three-page letter to the judge. Saying how this is not entirely his fault, and he needs help, and I need help—on and on to the judge. It was very impressive. And the judge basically says, 'I had every intention of sending you to prison this morning. But, in light of the victim's testimony, I'm gonna give you a halfway house sentence.'

"So, I was in the halfway house. I got a nine-year halfway house sentence. They actually put me in a… It's called the Intensive Residential Treatment program in county jail. It's kind of a court ordered treatment type thing. I've been through several treatment facilities, so it's nothing new to me. And they allow us to get out and, you know, go to the library and stuff like that. Well, I got on the computers in the library, and I couldn't contact her on Facebook, but I could see how she's doing. And there's a picture of our dog that she posted on her Facebook page, and I wasn't thinking. My attorney had said, 'Do not contact her on Facebook. They monitor that shit.' I didn't believe it. I believe it now because I 'liked' the picture of our dog on her Facebook page, and that violated the protection order.

"Anyway, off to prison I go. It wasn't like Pelican Bay or Sing Sing, or places like that. It was a minimum-restricted camp. I went to Four Mile first and that's where they kind of like, figure out what they're going to do with you. In the meantime, before you even get to your facility, you go through county jail— through Denver Reception Diagnostic Center. They assess you—IQ tests, mental health tests. And then they figure out where they're gonna house you for the rest of your sentence. They always do the alcohol questionnaires, and I know how to fill those out.

"But you know, at the time I was like, 'I'm done. It's fucking not funny anymore.' I filled out that I need help. So that goes in your record and then I was off to Four Mile for a while working at the dairy farm and back to dealing with cows—even in prison… What I was really wanting to get on was with the SWIFT program, 'cause I was wanting to do something in prison. I was not gonna do my time and whatever. I was going to try and, you know, put this to good use. I was wanting to get on the firefighting program—fight forest fires."

"What does SWIFT stand for?"

"Colorado has this State Wildland Inmate Fire Team. I've been running a chainsaw for years, and years, and years. And my military background, and everything else. And I thought I'd be a perfect candidate. But one morning they tell me to pack up. And I'm like, 'What the hell?'

"They're like, 'You're going to another facility.'

"'Ahhh… SWIFT… cool. I'm a badass.' The dumb shit you think of back then. But they dropped me off at another minimum restricted. And so that's where they have the

Therapeutic Community. And it sounds good. But it's the Department of Corrections treatment program they put offenders through if they have been diagnosed as needing drug and alcohol-type therapy. It's a year-long program, and you live it, you work it—day in, day out, and it's part of the daily routine. You gotta go to a job. They actually had a fishery—a tilapia fishery—so that's where I came up with how I wanna do my aquaponics stuff.

"But I went through that program. And it took me fifteen months to get through because I was like, really defiant. I still had that entitled, 'I'm a veteran. I'm a Ranger. I'm not like you guys. I'm not a drug dealer or gang member. I don't need to be here. All I need is AA.' And a lot of the therapists would really do serious manipulating with the inmates. You know, just trying to provoke stuff, so you could expose somebody's behavior. Because the whole thing was trying to raise someone's awareness of their behavior and their thinking errors. A lot of humbling experiences. But eventually, I got through it.

"The cool thing was that I was the AA Coordinator for the entire facility. Which means I was the guy that set up the meetings. I chaired the meetings. I made coffee. I was the 'AA Guy'. And that was frustrating but was still really rewarding. They just didn't get enough outside help, so we just had inmate meetings. I was talking to higher up the chain of command in the Department of Corrections—trying to get outside people, and it just fell on deaf ears. I'm just an inmate—or 'offender'. But for a long time, I was the 'AA Guy'… I chaired meetings. I ordered coins. I just did everything that I could while I was locked up. So that was good.

"Then eventually, you're there for a while… And the way it works in the Department of Corrections is that the longer you're there, the less of a threat you are. So, you have what's called, your Level of Security Index—your LSI report. So, as you complete all these other programs, like Seven Habits of Highly Effective People. That's like, really big in the Department of Corrections. And I went through that. And I still use all that stuff today, in addition to all the other therapy that I went through in the Therapeutic Community.

"Then I got transferred to this minimum camp, which was like Club Med. That's where the SWIFT crews are at. So, they have the nice gym, and the weight pile, and the nice yard. There's fucking trees. There's deer. I mean, you're literally feeding Raman noodles to deer at your window. These big bucks will just come up. Feed 'em apples and stuff like that. The COs are, 'Don't do that shit!'

"I'm, 'Whatever. Fuck you.' So, my defiance sometimes, too. You know? 'So, what are you gonna do to me? Put me in prison? I've already been there.' But it was kind of Club Med—you know, as far as prisons go.

"And then I was up for parole, working in the goat dairy. And they have all these operations to help inmates learn job skills, or whatever. Anyway, I've already completed the TC program, and I'm like, 'I'm outta here.' I've already been declined going to the halfway house once. And I was kind of ticked about that, but I was sure to get paroled. So, we go in—this was a video conference. It wasn't even actually a parole hearing. It was between my case manager and whoever's in charge of the parole hearing. I gave my speech. I took accountability. I admitted everything. You know, 'This is what I've done...'

"For whatever reason, he's like, 'With the seriousness of this offense, I don't think you need to be paroled.'

"And that just hit me like, 'What the fuck?! I've been a golden boy for like two and a half, three years!' And so that just hit me hard. I'm just like, 'Shit, I'm here for another year.' 'Cause, you don't see parole again for another year.

"Right after that, I went to my case manager. I was like, 'I want a fucking SWIFT application.' I filled that out to get on the inmate fire teams, and since I was there, I interviewed with the Fire Boss. And we did not like each other right off the bat. I had more experience. I had more leadership. Being an inmate firefighter is an ordeal all in itself. It's different politics and stuff like that. And the level of humility really starts to sink in. I mean it has to. I wasn't forced to, but I wanted to stay on the crew.

"I was actually the oldest guy… Well, no, my cellie was the oldest guy on the crew. Everybody else is in their twenties. And there's some guys that were just fucking animals. I'm still in pretty good shape, myself, but… So, I get on the fire crew, and this crew boss is just… I still got a resentment against the guy. I'm still working on it… It was humbling.

"Got through that fire season, and then I got paroled. While I was in, I was in the library studying aquaponics and wanting to make a greenhouse when I got out. You saw where that's at. The only thing to do was like… Mike was always sending me books and stuff—in the joint. And so, I had a plan. I had a really good plan—getting out… Run my tree service…

"I was really kind of disappointed when I paroled, that I couldn't find AA meetings around here. They just dried up. And this is even like, right pre-COVID. It was weird.

"This is kind of funny. 'Cause when I got out, I still had to get my driver's license reinstated. So, in order to do that, I had to finish taking the DUI classes that I started like, six years ago—so I had to take those fucking classes again. And we're sittin' there, goin' over the same shit that I went over for the last four years in that Therapeutic Community and all this other stuff. And I just kind of went in there, and I'm like, 'I'm not trying to impress anybody. I'm not trying to say I know anything. I'm just here because I have to be. But I got a lot of experience with this, so I'm just gonna do me.' The teacher was always calling on me. And it was just kind of, like, funny banter between me and her, and everybody. We all had to be there, but we didn't have to be shitty about it. Just tryin' to make it fun, and stuff like that. So that was like my weekly kind of meeting, almost. So that got me through, but my drive has been trying to get this tree business goin'. That's been my thing, and right now… it's doin' good."

"So, you've been working on your business since you got out?"

"Mmm-hmm… I worked my ass off last year. I just flat worked myself to the bone. This time last year, my fingernails were falling off. I'd been climbing so much rope—climbing trees. I worked so much it was just unreal. Just dealing with adversity. You know? Roadblocks life throws at you, and you just overcome 'em. Nothing special.

"I just got out, and I didn't have as much AA support as I wanted to. I still always talked to Mike. I'm still kind of like, working the program. I don't pick up the Big Book as often as I need to. I'm focused more on living life. Because I lost out on so much of that. You know? It's like, the hardest thing for me to hear was, listening to my mom on the prison fucking phone telling me, 'You had so much potential.' Past tense. You know?

"When you get put in there, and you have few choices. You have very little control of anything other than how you think. And I did learn a lot of good stuff in that Therapeutic Community. I was defiant, but I learned from it. It was necessary for me to be where I am right now. And right now, it's really cool.

"I have a girlfriend that's awesome. I'm my own boss. I make really good money. And I'm doing something I love. I'm part of a community again. And that's fuckin' huge for me. Because the people here, they don't remember 'Brad the drunk.' They don't remember the 'gutter bravado'. It's not something I'm ashamed of, but it's not something I wear like a badge of honor. It's just another chapter in my life."

"It sounds like you're just ready to move on."

"I'm done. I have moved on. Where I'm at now is, I'm workin' my ass off. Trying to find balance in life. I know I'm one drink away from a drunk. I can't put myself up on a pedestal. I can't let my ego get into my head. I still have to check my motives. You know, I work a program without really thinkin' about it. It's a self-supporting kind of program and sometimes I need other frickin' nuts to talk to, and stuff like that. I think that's one of Mike's sayings, 'If you're talking to yourself, you're talking to a nut.'

"I got out, and I was fortunate. I got out of prison with a nice little bank account. And was able to buy a vehicle and stuff like that. I started with the tree climbing gear that Mike held onto for me. I had it in a storage unit and he brought it down here. It was waiting for me before I even got out of prison. That's all I had. I don't have much now, but I have a lot of peace of mind. If I allow myself that peace of mind. Sometimes I'm my own worst critic. Frequently I am. But all my needs are met.

"I was thinking about that the other day. I have people that I did jobs for two weeks ago that owe me thousands of dollars. And I put off billing that out just because it's either in their bank account or mine. It doesn't really matter. They're gonna pay me. That whole— 'Fear of people and of economic insecurity will leave us.'[6] I was just driving down the road the other day, and I was like, 'Where the fuck did that come from?' The promises… I always remember that. That's just kind of where I'm at. I've made the serious amends that I need to. I make living amends every day. I always try to do something for family, community, friends. I do a lot of stuff nobody knows about. I don't need to be in the paper.

"I'm blessed. But in the end, I work my fucking ass off. I used the time that I had when I was in prison. I can design aquaponic systems, and that's just like a hobby for me to go relax. But as far as, like, my business goes—I deal with employee issues and stuff like that. But that's my drive. It's just, be a better person than I was yesterday. It's not about being the biggest and the best, or the smartest, or the strongest, or anything. It's just to be better than who I was. I fall short a lot. A lot. But you know, that's just where I'm at.

"I'm definitely, you know, a friend of Bill and Bob—a student of Bill and Bob.[13] There's a lot of books that I really get into like, *Dr. Bob and the Good Oldtimers* and a lot of the history about AA, and stuff like that. And I get a lot of that from Mike. He's worn off on me so much. It's weird. He's a good guy, though.

"It works, but it's a lot of work. And that's one of the things I was tryin' to express when I was still doin' these DUI classes that I had to do and talk to all these other people. I mean, the shit works. You can do it. Simple… It's not easy, and it's fucking a lot of work and it's a lot of discipline."

"I do have some questions if you don't mind. Some pretty pointed questions, just to clarify some things."

"OK."

---

[13] This is a reference to Bill Wilson and Dr. William D. Silkworth (Dr. Bob), co-founders of Alcoholics Anonymous.

"Did you ever do drugs?"

"Not really. I mean, smokin' pot, but that wasn't anything."

"Most of the guys I talked to had a really hard time in prison—they got their asses beat. What was time in prison like for you?"

"I had to get stitched up a few times in the joint, too. But, you know, there's a lot of stuff that I don't want to, like— Again, that 'gutter bravado'. I don't wanna glamorize it. For me, now it's kind of like, I don't have to— Somethin' changed that I just don't have to... I don't have to try and impress people anymore."

"How much time did you do in prison?"

"Four and a half years."

"And if you were to add up, like all of your time in jails and prison, how much of your life do you think you've been locked up?"

"Five years. You know, like all that time in county jail here, or thirty days in county jail there. I mean, I met some guys that got their number in the '60s—the 1960's—and they're still walking the yard. It's not the amount of time that you do, it's what happens or what you do with the time that you're in... I think."

"That's a good point. If you had something to say about sobriety and about life once you get out, to people that are there right now, what would that be?"

"There is a solution. You know, definitely, there is a solution. It's not easy, and there's gonna be obstacles. And there's gonna be adversity. And you're gonna have to deal with it every day. You know, it's dealing with life on life's terms, and that's all it is. It's what you hear in meetings forever. Shit happens. You know, I don't get Internet in my greenhouse. Oh well. You know? It's nothing to get fuckin' stupid and kick the dog over. Going back to the promises, this whole, 'We will intuitively know how to handle situations which used to baffle us.'[6] You know, I do that all the time. And I'm just like, 'How did I not lose my shit over that instance right there?' It's free for the taking, yet so few people take it. It's hard. You know, I'm not going to sugarcoat shit. But it's feasible, and so worth it, and so rewarding.

"What I've built with my life in the last eighteen months, is what I tried so hard to build for that fifteen years prior. So that fifteen years of me struggling with the fucking bottle—it was all my alcoholism. And I've been to treatment—I mean, if you want to count the stuff in prison—four separate times. Four DUI arrests, two DUI convictions, and it's all over fucking drinking. And I see it now, like, a lot of my other behaviors. I drink the shit out of Monster energy drinks. But I'm not gonna go to jail over the stupid stuff I do on Monsters. You know?

"I don't know where that drive came from. I don't know where my spiritual awakening happened, or how it happened, or when

.t happened. Maybe I'm more of the educational variety. I don't know. I think about stuff sometimes. I don't question why. I'm just glad the results are working."

"How do you deal with stuff today, since you don't drink?"

"I find it in my greenhouse. My family. My girlfriend. My dog. I can go fishing and catch some bass."

"What does your Higher Power look like today?"

"It's not the Higher Power, it's not the God, it's not Jesus that I was baptized to. It's the Intelligent Creator of the universe. I've read a lot of physics and Stephen Hawking, and I don't understand any of it. But there is something there.

"One of the things that I kind of got into when I was in the joint, and this was like one of the things I was into when I was in the Army, as well. A lot of soldiers kind of go this route. They kind of get into the old Norse Paganism—with Odin and Thor and stuff like that. And it's a simple explanation for me. I'm more of a hippie, dirt-loving paganistic kind of guy. For me, I love being up in the fucking tree. And sometimes it's just like—this is my church. I find it in nature. I find it in just noticing something other than myself. When I'm with trees... I commune with my Higher Power every day.

"Like the promises, like I was talking about earlier, '...sometimes quickly, sometimes slowly. They will always materialize…'[6] But you gotta work your ass off for it. It's not easy. But it's fuckin' worth it!"

In Other Words…

"My name is Tom Richardson, and I am an atheist alcoholic."

In the rooms of AA, most members will introduce themselves using just their first name. And rarely will someone mention a certain religion or lack thereof. Consequently, some are put off by his brazen announcement as we circle the room.

"Introducing yourself that way pisses some people off," I once remarked.

"Fuck 'em," he said.

Surprisingly, Tom is well-versed in the Bible and other sacred texts. When pressed about why he chooses to leave when the meeting closes with The Lord's Prayer, he'll point out that it's a Christian prayer, and AA is not a religious organization. Further, Tom interprets the Bible to give clear instructions to believers in Matthew 6:6, which reads, "But when you pray, go into your room, close the door and pray to your Father, who is unseen. Then your Father, who sees what is done in secret, will reward you." (New International Version). So I ask myself, should the prayer be expressed in a group setting? I see sound reasoning in his assertion. And for a while, I'm reluctant to participate in the tradition that some groups have to close meetings with that prayer.

Though Tom is unwavering with his views, on more than one occasion, I've heard him say,

> "The problem with the world today is that most people don't practice Christian values. Now, I'm an atheist. But I still practice Christian values."

Boldly broaching controversial topics, he holds his own in the face of backlash. He'll openly proclaim his political affiliation and voice unpopular opinions.

> "I can be a real asshole and I'm proud of it."

Still, he is well-liked.

Over the years, I've learned a lot from Tom. He takes life in stride with an enviable sense of humor. In a meeting one day, he talked about a time when a hidden bag of pruno burst in the ductwork of the prison, in which he was detained. Apparently, holes poked in the bag were too small for fermentation gases to escape. The explosion, and ensuing room toss, took place while Tom was in solitary confinement.

> "I could tell you so many hilarious stories about prison life, you could write a book."

Little did he know… As I toil away with this project, I keep thinking of that story and his comment. It comes at a point in my interviewing process when portrayals of prison life deeply disturb me. I realize it's imperative I include his slant on things. So, the next time I see him, I pitch my idea.

We sneak out of the club, while others are forming a circle to close the meeting with The Lord's Prayer. His polished trike poses in a spot marked "Handicapped." Nowadays, he'll often opt for the stability of three wheels instead of riding his two-wheeled Harleys. He hasn't fully recovered from his wreck, and perhaps never will. Ironically, he was hit by a drunk driver. Though his injuries have aged him, Tom still makes an entrance with a smile. He's a jovial man wearing dark shades, holding a cigarette, and basking in the sun. We frequently smoke and talk, relaxing in the old ratty lawn chairs that border the building.

Today, he straddles his motorcycle instead. I want to explain everything about the book before anyone opens the door, so I talk fast. Throughout my spiel, he calmly nods. He likes the concept and agrees to contribute. I'm thrilled.

"I won't use your real name," I assure him.

> "I don't care. You can call me 'asshole' if you want." He grins
> and takes a drag.

Shortly afterward, we meet via Zoom. In his home, he reclines with his leg elevated, and is periodically distracted by pain. I try to be quick, which will cost us in the long run—I end up asking for four additional sessions to collect all the information I need.

"Why do you introduce yourself using your full name and stressing that you are an atheist?"

"I started using my full name a long time back when I used to introduce myself as Tattoo Tom. You know, which—my biker name. And then somebody came up and said, 'Well, I tried to call ya the other night, but I couldn't find 'Tattoo Tom' in the phone book.' So, I started using my whole name because anonymity at the level of press, radio, and films does not mean we have to have anonymity in these rooms.[14]

"And I introduce myself as atheist because there are a lot of people who, when they first come to this program, are not... The word 'God' scares 'em off, a lot. So, I introduce myself as an atheist to let people know that they may not be alone in these rooms. The other day I had some guy, after a meeting, come up to me and shake my hand and say, 'Thank you, Tom. I am too.' You know, so that's why I do that."

Though Tom and I have different perspectives when it comes to spirituality, we've spent plenty of time respectfully exchanging ideas. At one point, he established a local 12 Step recovery group named after a larger fellowship called, "Freethinkers." Sheer curiosity led me to sit in on some of their meetings. Atheist, agnostic, religious, spiritual. It didn't matter. All were welcome. Meetings were basically the same as any other 12 Step recovery meeting, except when they adjourned

---

[14] The eleventh tradition of Alcoholics Anonymous states, "Our public relations policy is based on attraction rather than promotion; we need always maintain personal anonymity at the level of press, radio, and films." This can be found along with the other short-form traditions in the Big Book on page 562 of the 4th edition.

people simply got up, pushed in their chairs, and left. There was no closing prayer. Sadly, the local group never really took off. But the larger body flourishes. The "Freethinkers" community identifies itself as a secular, non-religious expression of Alcoholics Anonymous. Members practice non-theist adaptations of the Twelve Steps.

I ask Tom, "Do you use an alternative 12 Step book that's similar to the Big Book?"

"Yes. I have several books that I read, just like they have *As Bill Sees It,* and *One Day at a Time,* and all that. I have several books on my phone that I have gotten off of Amazon. One of those being, *The Alternative Twelve Steps and Traditions*. And it lists, oh shit, probably about eight or nine of 'em in the book. And I do—though I'm not religious—I do have on my phone [an app] where I get these, sort of like *Daily Reflections* from Buddhism, because they don't mention a God. They just say things like, '*You* are responsible for your actions and what happens in your life.' Not some deity."

"How did you find those books? Did someone introduce you to them?"

"I found those on the Internet. 'Cause I was going to this one site that was for agnostics and atheists, and that's where I learned about the alternative Steps. And there are so many different ones. There's a Buddhist one, and an agnostic one, you know. So, I researched it and I read 'em all. I put together, actually, the Steps from several different lists. And uh, started working that. But I found all that stuff online."

I find myself repeatedly challenging Tom, trying to get him to admit there has to be some sort of Higher Power. But he won't budge.

"Do you have a Higher Power, or is it all on you?"

> "No, it's like when they say the Serenity Prayer, I say, '*I* grant me the serenity to accept the things I cannot change.'"

"Is it fair to say that you find a Higher Power in the group?"

> "No, because I really don't believe in *any* Higher Power. Including myself. Yeah, there's something in the universe, but I don't consider it to be a Higher Power."

"Do you think there's a Creator of the Universe that gave this energy and put out galaxies?"

> "I believe in the Big Bang Theory."

"How do you explain the Big Bang? It didn't just come out of nowhere."

> "I can't explain it. But scientifically, I'm sure there's a way. I'm sure it was a couple of molecules that were just floating around and collided and caused the Big Bang. Like, I know that when you have two things collide and you have a Big Boom, it all spreads out to make the big universe. But eventually, it'll stop spreading out and start going back in. And then eventually, we'll have another Big Bang… This takes more time than I can even think of."

"It's hard to fathom."

"Yeah."

"Were you an atheist when you came into the rooms?"

"No, I was kind of agnostic when I came in."

"What made you turn to atheism?"

"That's a long story. But pretty much, just from all the hypocrites—people in church and people in AA. You know? I'd go to AA for my drinking problem, and me and a couple guys would go out and pack our nose afterwards. And then I'd go to NA for the coke problem, and we'd go out for a beer afterwards.

"When did your drinking and drugging career begin?"

"I had my first acid trip when I was ten years old. This was in the early '60s."

"Would you say that you graduated [substances]? Like, when did you start smoking cigarettes?"

"OK… I used to… when I'd speak at speaker meetings, I would start out by saying that I started smokin' cigarettes when I was six years old. I had my first hit of acid when I was ten. And if you ask me when I had my first drink of alcohol, all I could tell ya is my mother believed that if a baby wouldn't quit crying, put a little wine in his bottle and he'd go right to sleep. And then there was all the poker games and stuff at the house, where... yeah... I was runnin' around, drinkin' beer."

"What were your parents like as far as drugs and alcohol go?"

"Yeah, well, drinkers. My father died from emphysema. 'Cause I 'member goin' up to Alaska. My mother called me and said, 'You need to come up 'cause your father's in the hospital, and he's not gonna be comin' out.'

"So, I went up there and walked in his room... [He said,] 'Good to see ya, Boy! Gimme a fuckin' cigarette!'

"But my mother... I think it was basically she didn't wanna live without my father." She passed just three months later.

"Do you have any siblings?"

"Two brothers. One older, one younger."

"Did your brothers get into trouble, too?"

"Nope. I was the only one. I was the middle child. And the middle child is usually the one."

"Middle kids are always trouble."

"Yep."

Back in the day, Tom hung out with one-percenters. "You got in a lot of trouble when you were drinking... I remember you saying you'd go out with your friends, and they'd say, 'Who's gonna fight the little fucker tonight?'"

"Yeah, that was in a biker bar in Alaska. Because when I was drinking, I was six foot tall, three hundred and fifty pounds— just like every fuckin' biker in the bar. I never won a fight, but I got my fuckin' ass kicked a lot."

"When did you start getting into trouble?"

"I was fifteen. And I got kicked out of junior high, and they put me in the high school because the junior high kids were too afraid of me."

"Why were they afraid of you?"

"OK… 'Cause that's back when… I can't 'member the name of the movie now—but the Socs and the Greasers. Yeah, well I was a Greaser. I've got pictures someplace, back in that time, where I was wearing a motorcycle jacket and had the greased back hair. So, most of the kids were afraid of me. I was a bully. And you know, drinking and doin' drugs. That was in Walnut Creek, California, which is just behind Oakland. We'd always go into Berkeley. And… Yeah, that was during the Summer of Love in San Francisco. All I remember is the Berkeley riots."

"Because you were so messed up?"

"Yeah."

"What do you think led you down the path of drinking, and drugging, and getting into trouble?"

"One of my first memories is my father coming home drunk and gettin' in a fight with my mother. And wound up dragging her out in the front yard by her hair in her nightgown. And the cops comin' and haulin' him off. They never divorced. They were together right up until they both passed away. But yeah, that, and bein' an army brat. You know? We moved around a lot. So, I never made close friends. I always was hesitant around other people. And I started drinking at a really young age.

"And then we moved from there up to Washington. 'Cause California and Washington are totally different universes. I wound up getting in trouble, and the school said the only way I could get back in was if my parents sent me to Western State Mental Institution as a day patient. So, I had to go to school there, with all the nut cases."

"I remember you ended up running away from that institution with another kid. What happened when you ran away? Where did you go?"

"We went up and stayed with some friends of his, up in Tacoma. One day we were sitting there watching TV and heard a commotion down in the parking lot. Looked out and there were four cop cars there. So, I was told to go hide in the shower. Next thing I know, a cop throws the damn curtain across, and grabs me by the neck, and throws me down."

"Did they take you back to the institution or did they take you home?"

"No, I went to juvenile hall. I was there for about a month and then they let me out. My father was up in Alaska at that time, so they let me out to go up and stay with him. I was basically kicked out of the state of Washington... Well, they didn't really kick me out, I guess. They told my mother they would let me out of juvenile hall if she would send me up to Alaska to be with my father."

"And how old were you then?"

"About fifteen... Yeah. 'Cause when I was waitin' to catch a plane to go up to Alaska to be with my father, my mother and I sat down and looked at a map. And she had figured we'd been in all forty-eight contiguous states."

"So, you went to high school in Anchorage and dropped out. You've said that that's when it [the addiction] 'was on.' Did you get a GED later?"

"Later on, I did, in Iowa."

"How old were you then?"

"Let's see, probably thirty-five... Thirty-four or thirty-five."

"So that was right before you got clean and sober?"

"Yeah."

"So, what is your sobriety date?"

"I'll have thirty-three years next March."

"I bet you'd created a lot of wreckage in your past before that."

"This friend of mine was a cop, and when I was having a problem getting a truck driving job, I asked him to run an NCIC check on me."[15]

"What's that?"

"I can't remember now… But at any rate, he called me back a few days later and says, 'Damn! You had a lot of fuckin' fun in the '70s, didn't ya?!'"

"I remember, you said you had a bunch of 'Public Intoxications'."

"Intoxication, Possession of Stolen Firearms…"

"Stolen Firearms? Tell me that story."

"I thought I told you this story… Well, we'd gone up to… I can't remember exactly where we were going. We were going up a highway and we turned down this road right next to a lodge. And we got the car stuck. So, me and another guy walked back up to the lodge. And they had what's called a 'Booda.' And it's just a vehicle that has a cab here and a cab here. You know, so you can go either which way."

---

[15] The NCIC (National Crime Information Center) is a nationwide computerized information system for all criminal justice agencies.

"It was called a 'Booda'?"

"They had a lot at the airports in Alaska and my dad called them 'Boodas'… So, we hot-wired it and took it. And the manager of the lodge woke up just as we were takin' it and called the police. And we went out, and there was this cabin right where the car was stuck. And we broke into the cabin and stole a whole bunch of guns. We were pulled over two weeks later."

"Oh yeah… And that was with the judge."

"Uh-huh… Yep, the judge's cabin."

"So, what happened when you got caught?"

"A couple of my friends took responsibility for it and told the cops that I didn't have any. So, I got thirty days in jail and then I was let out."

"The last time you were in jail was for your second and third DUI. Is that right?"

"Second and third DUI, fifth and sixth Driving on a Suspended License."

"Did you have any felonies?"

"State felonies, not federal felonies."

"Was that for the Sale of Narcotics? I remember you mentioning that."

"I got busted. I was less than six months on probation from a drug charge when I got pulled over for Driving While

Intoxicated, Possession of Marijuana, and Possession of Amphetamines. That was when my friend Pete—he came up and told the cop, 'Well, you know, they're getting ready to legalize pot in Alaska.'

"'Cause, they had legalized it for a while back in the '70s. Then it became illegal again, and now it's legal…

"But Pete says to the cop, 'I can drive him home. I know he's had a few too many to drink. But I can drive him home.'

"The cop says, 'Well I'm gonna look around a little bit more.' Reaches into the car and pulls out this jar.

"And Pete says, 'What the fuck is that?'

"I said, 'Well if I'm not mistaken, that's a jar of methamphetamine. That's five hundred hits.' So, I didn't go home that night."

"So that was when you caught a felony for Sale of Narcotics?"
"Uh… No, that was before. And I was on probation for that. And yeah… So, it was basically… They rolled into one."

"OK… Do you wanna explain it?"
"Well, it's been so long it's hard to explain. Uh, basically I think what it was, was after the first one, I was put on

Imposition of Sentence—which means that [if] I stayed clean for four or five years, then I wouldn't have a felony on my record. But getting popped with the hits of methamphetamine—I wound up with a felony."

"And you ended up in jail. Or was it prison?"

"Well, it was Wildwood Correctional Facility. I went there for a year."[16]

"You once shared an experience you had while you were there... Prison life—you were given something to pass on. And you found out later that it was a file."

"Mmm-hmm. And the guy that got the file broke out of jail with it."

"And then he killed your friend?"

"No, he didn't kill him. He just shot him. And after I'd gotten out, I saw him at a meeting, and I told him exactly what had happened. And he said, 'Don't worry about it.' He says, 'I understand. You were in jail. You did what you had to do to stay alive.'"

---

[16] According to its website, Wildwood Correctional Center is "... a medium custody long-term sentenced facility, which houses adult male felon and misdemeanor prisoners of medium and minimum custody levels."

"Because you have to do what you have to do to survive in the penitentiary, do you think it's possible to practice the principles of the program while you're there?"[4]

"No. That last time at Wildwood Correctional Facility, I had a year sober when I went in, 'cause I had gotten the DWI and all that shit. And it took a lot of time in court. But I had a year when I went in. And, I was in two weeks, and I was dirty."

"How did that happen? Why?"

"Boredom. Pure boredom. And there's a lot of drugs. And like I said, pruno—in prison. You know, there's always somethin' to get fucked up on."

"Right…" I refer to notes I took earlier. "You told me you had tattoos done while you were in prison."

"Yep, every one of these is coverin' up an old jail tattoo or a street tattoo."

"One of the things that I've found interesting, is all the ingenious ways people do tattoos when they're in there. How did they do them when you were there?"

"OK, the old cassette players and stuff…"

"The Walkmans?"

"Yeah, that's what it was. You take the motor out. And then you use an ink pen barrel and then a paper clip. And then the motor would do the paper clip and then you always had ink pens. And that's how you do the jail tattoos."

"How do you do it without getting caught?"

"During the daytime, you could roam around, go into other people's rooms, stuff like that. And so, you'd go in, get a tattoo done. Somebody would be out in the hallway and knock on the door and let you know when a guard was comin' that way."

"In prison, did you do anything that you were proud of? Or did you just do your time?"

"I tried to stay in solitary confinement."

"Was that for protection reasons?"

"No, just because I didn't wanna be around the assholes in prison."

"Did you have any contact with gangs while you were in there?"

"No. In Alaska, there were hardly any gangs. You know? I mean, you had the Hell's Angels, which in the early years was the Brothers of Alaska. But then they were dissolved and became Hell's Angels. But other than that, back in the '70s, there wasn't that much gang activity. It was only in New York and Los Angeles… Chicago."

"How many times would you say you've been in jail?"

"Oh fuck, I can't count how many times. Drunk in Public and Disorderly Conduct and shit."

"How much time would you say that you did in jails and penitentiaries—total over your life?"

"Four years."

"And how much of that was straight-time?"

"Just one year."

"That's enough…"

"Well and that was, you know, after that third DUI and sixth— driving with my license suspended. The judge sent me to prison for a year and told me that… He guaranteed me that if I got stopped again, I'd be doing more than two years. Which means I would be shipped out of Alaska and sent to McNeil Island in Seattle, Washington. And they've closed it down since then."

"Do you know why?"

"No, I don't think I ever cared to know why. You can probably Google it."

"OK, so you went from juvenile hall to going in and out of jail, then spent a year in prison."

"Most of it was involving drugs and alcohol and doing stupid shit while I was drunk or high."

"When you say, 'stupid shit', what do you mean? What's an example of that?"

"Um, fighting, Petty Larceny and shit like that."

"Petty Larceny? What did you do?"

"Maybe steal a few bucks from somebody. Basically theft."

"So, you didn't get in a lotta big trouble, but you stayed in trouble your whole life until you got clean and sober?"

"Yeah."

"What made you leave the life that you were leading to get clean and sober? What was your motivation?"

"Just tired of… You know, I was homeless back in the '70s. Up in Alaska during the wintertime when it got down to twenty below, you just grab a big rock, throw it through a business window and you get three hots and a cot for thirty days."

"At one point, when you were going in and out of jail, a judge sent you to AA. That was your introduction to 12 Step recovery, right?"

"Yeah."

"But you were getting drunk in prison."

"I bounced in and out [of AA] for close to fifteen years. I was just having problems accepting everything. And, you know, with the religion thing. There was a time, up in Alaska, where it seemed like everybody that was in the program was a

Catholic. So, I figured I couldn't be an alcoholic, 'cause I wasn't Catholic."

"So, is that why it took fifteen years to get settled in the program? Because you were thinking it was a religion?"

"Well, that and a lot of other things, really. I mean, I knew I had a drinking problem. And everybody told me I had a drinking, and drugging problem. But I wasn't really willing to— Well, I guess I accepted it. But I just wasn't ready to quit... is what it amounts to.

"I 'member after my last year in prison, my sponsor came and picked me up. And uh, took me out to a bar for a drink."

"Oh really?"

"Yeah, he let me drink and he drank Coke. But he said, 'You know, Tom, you aren't ever gonna stay sober if you stay in Alaska. So, we both left Alaska. We left the majestic mountains of Alaska for the cornfields of Iowa. He got me back on my feet and said, 'Well Tom, I'm going back up to Alaska. Don't you ever fuckin' come back!' 'Cause he knew I wouldn't stay sober up there.

"So, I stayed sober... maybe six months or so. Then I went and got drunk again. And then I was in the program, again. But I got a job with an outfit that went around the country putting up these mini-storage warehouses. And we bounced around from

Florida, South, North Carolina, all the way back across the country to Portland, Oregon. I stayed sober for a while.

"Somewhere along the line, I decided the kids— You know, there were about five of us, and we went by pick-up everywhere. And we were all staying in a motel. Then after work, everybody wanted to go to the bar, drinkin'. Guys would have their drinks and I drank my Coke. And somewhere along the line I just… Those kids didn't know how to drink. I had to show 'em. And that brought back the cocaine—I lost the job."

"Sounds like you did a lot of coke back then, too."

"One morning, I'd been partying all night and I was still all coked up. And I was sittin' there, readin' the newspaper about this guy that OD'd on cocaine. And I'm sittin' there, like this [trembling]. My heart's poundin'. I was just gettin' ready to overdose and didn't even fuckin' know it. 'Nobody can overdose on cocaine. What the fuck is this shit?!'"

"So, what did you do?"

"Just rode it out and went on through my day."

"What made the program click for you after having bounced in and out for fifteen years? What did your bottom look like?"

"I finally just got sick and tired of bein' sick and tired. You know, of going in and out of jail and mental institutions—for attempted suicide and all kinds of weird shit. Yeah, I just finally had enough."

"So, it sounds like you were finally willing to deal with what you thought was a religious organization, 'cause you knew there was recovery there. Is that what happened?"

"Yes, because I've been an atheist ever since then. It was basically I'd learned to deal, lettin' the religious shit go in one ear and then out the other. And working the program the way I needed to work it—so that it worked for me."

"Before AA, had you tried to quit drinking and drugging on your willpower?"

"Oh yeah… Didn't work at all. I mean, early on in the program… You know, 'cause the first fifteen years—bouncing in and out of the program. I couldn't… Yeah, it just wasn't clicking. 'Cause I'd go to AA meetings and afterwards go out and have a beer. You know? Or go out with a couple of guys and pack my nose with coke. And then I'd go to NA, and afterwards would go out and have a beer… Back in the early '70s, for some reason, a lot of people went to NA and just went out and drank a beer afterwards."

"So, you've been to both Narcotics Anonymous and Alcoholics Anonymous?"

"Actually, just last night I went to an NA meeting. First time since probably 2005. Probably be the last time in my life. I don't care for NA"

"I didn't either. I don't know why. I just feel at home in AA."

"Yeah, so do I."

"If you tried quitting drinking and drugging on your own willpower and that didn't work, what worked? What happened? What made it stick for you, if not a Higher Power?"

"Basically, the last time I went out [relapsed], I started seeing a psychologist. And she saw to it that I got on Prozac. Because I've been on antidepressants since I was fifteen. And I'd take 'em for a while. Things would be great. And I'd quit taking 'em and, you know, go right back. 'Cause I was diagnosed as being a manic depressive with antisocial tendencies. Today they call it bipolar— 'cause it sounds better. But she got me back on 'em and I've been on 'em ever since. And I attribute that to my being able to accept the fact that I'm powerless and I don't wanna be anymore."

"Then, you probably don't subscribe to the philosophy some have, that any type of mind-altering substance isn't okay in AA."

"No. Because I can say that without Prozac, I probably wouldn't have thirty-two years. You know, 'cause I'd get so depressed that I'd be back to drugs and alcohol."

"Do you have a sponsor?"

"We co-sponsor each other—Max and I do. 'Cause we've known each other for, shit, going on twenty-five years. And uh, he's got thirty-three, got thirty-four, comin' up. And I've got thirty-two, so we basically co-sponsor each other."

"Do you sponsor other people?"

"I have… You know Jerry? He has thrown a couple of people my way—that are having a problem with the 'God thing'. Basically, I don't advertise that I'm willing to sponsor, but if anybody should approach me and say, 'Well you know I'm having a problem with the 'God thing', 'cause I'm more atheist…' Then I will share my experience, strength, and hope with them. And help them through."

"What else do you do as far as service work goes?"

"Today, not a whole lot. I have been on the committee for the conference for three years. But basically, pretty much since my accident I've been isolating."

"How does that affect your program?"

"Not bad because, you know Max is living at my house, so we sit and talk a lot."

Forgetting that Tom doesn't follow the actual Big Book of AA, I ask him, "If you have no Higher Power, how were you able to achieve the psychic change that the Big Book talks about?"

"OK, that's where— I believe that… You know, a lot of people in the program are religious. And they believe in Jesus. Or a lot of them will say, 'Higher Power'. And that's fine. But with me? I mean, there was a time when I was agnostic. But now I'm not. I'm definitely atheist. And I believe that with this vast universe… The universe is made up of atoms and molecules and that's what we are. We're atoms and molecules. And so, therefore I know that when this life is over my atoms 'n' molecules will become something else. I don't know what. You know? But it definitely has nothing to do with a God or a Higher Power. It's how the universe is."

"OK… Besides staying alive, what other benefits are there to being clean and sober?"

"Just basically being able to get along with people. And uh… Not to be sad and in self-pity all the time. Enjoy life."

"You've become a successful entrepreneur. To what do you owe your success?"

"Uh… Ed Rogers. He's the one that taught me drafting. And after I'd learned and started my own business, Ed and I had our offices in the same office… So, Ed—I credit a lot for my entrepreneurship… Yeah. 'Cause I did that for fourteen years. No… longer than that. A lot longer than that. 'Cause I was employed with an architectural firm, and I worked there for thirteen years before I started truck driving. And then I got tired of working for somebody else truck driving. So, I bought my own truck and trailer and got my own authority."[17]

"At one point, you told me that you had some hilarious stories you could tell me about being in prison. Will you tell me one?"

"When I was locked up in Anchorage Alaska, I was in the shower, and somebody poured cold water over the wall on me. And I came running out and I had soap in my eyes. And I just started swingin' at the first person that I came to. And I wiped the soap outta my eyes and there was this big fuckin' black dude. And uh, I looked at him and said, 'You know, I imagine you'll beat the shit out of me, but I guarantee I'm gonna bite your fucking nuts off on my way down!' And he just laughed and walked away."

"OK, last question. What would you tell someone who's struggling with alcohol?"

"I would say that you do not need to go through what I went through. But if you do, just remember—you fall down, you get up, you eat your pride, and you come back to these rooms, and you start over again. And I can't stress enough—you need to talk about your past with somebody. Whether it be somebody in the program—like a closed-mouthed sponsor, or a clergyman. Or, you know, just a drunk on the corner.

---

[17] "Authority," is the permission granted by the Federal Motor Carriers Safety Administration (FMCSA) to transport goods for profit.

"I mean, last week we had a memorial for someone who had just committed suicide a couple of weeks ago because he was not able to deal with his past. But nobody in these rooms knew about it, because he hid it so well. So yeah, you've gotta talk about your past. If it's troubling you, especially. You deal with somebody that's closed-mouthed—that won't talk behind your back or say anything to anybody else. And there are people like that in this program. You know, me being one. Somebody tells me something—I'm gonna hold it in confidence. Someone telling me about their past and what's bothering 'em about their past will help me to tell them, 'Hey, you're not alone. I fuckin' went through all that shit myself.' So yeah, I can't stress enough—you have to be honest with yourself and talk about it. No matter how bad things get, it turns out okay in the end if you just hang in there."

Breaking the Bars Within

"I don't know exactly what next week looks like. But I'll tell you what, I know I'm gonna be okay. I know that God's gonna give me exactly what I need when I need it. You know why I can say I know? Because he's done it for me this last five years. Ever since I had a change of heart."

lmost unrecognizable, beaming as he walks by. So different from what I remember…

Years ago, I'd sometimes see Rob at a Sunday meditation meeting across town. He'd be running late, hurrying through the path of people to get to a recliner in the back. Its massive cushions swallowed him as he dove into it. He looked sad. Troubled. With a flat voice, he'd hint at hardships—omitting specifics and staring at the floor. Had it not been for us circling the room for shares, would he have said anything at all?

But now here he is, smiling and talking about gratitude. It's not so much what he says. It's the way he says it—using lively gestures. I turn to a friend and comment on this remarkable transformation. "You should ask him to be in your book," she says.

After the meeting, he sticks around for hugs and handshakes. I wait until he finishes visiting with the other members, then ask him for a moment of his time. I fill him in on the project, trying to gauge his interest. He seems flattered and humbly agrees to schedule an interview.

"I'll call you as soon as I get home," I say. "That way, I'll have my planner in front of me. Will you be free for a while?"

"Yeah, I was just gonna head over to the gym."

In less than an hour, Rob agrees to be a contributor.

"It might take some work to get me to open up. But once I get started— I have so much to be grateful for. And I know it's just gonna keep getting better."

Several weeks pass before I capture his hope—when we sit down to talk via Zoom.

"You ready?" I ask.

"I suppose."

"We're just gonna have a casual conversation. We'll cover, like I said, stuff we would in a speaker meeting. You know—what it was like, what happened, what it's like now. I'll just ask you questions as we go."

"Alright."

"So why don't you start by telling me a little bit about your family? What was it like for you growing up?"

"Well, I had an older brother and sister. My brother was just one year older than me. And then my mom raised us. My dad passed away two weeks before I turned two years old. He died of hypothermia. He had gotten lost on a hunting trip. So that's what happened to him.

"Growing up, it was just us three kids and my mom. Things were cool growin' up, other than my mom used to abuse us. She could get pretty violent at times. She didn't hold back. She used to— She would smack us around with whatever was close—rakes, hangers. All that good stuff. But you know, she loved us. She just was under a lot of stress. Come to find out, as I was an adult, she didn't have the best childhood either. So, it is what it is, there.

"I grew up playin' sports up until ninth grade when I injured my knee. But, drinkin' and smokin' weed was normal in my whole family, pretty much—from a young age. Used to hang out at my dad's parents' house a lot, with my uncles. And that side of the family, and in that environment, smokin' weed and drinkin' was normal. So that's what I grew up doin'."

"So, were you pretty little when you started that then?"

"Oh, smokin' and drinkin'? Oh yeah. At least as young as junior high—that I can think back.

"But you know, my mom did real good supporting us. We always had a home. We always had a vehicle. We always had a washer and dryer in the house. She took care of us. And she was always the loudest parent at our sports games—cheering us on. So, I'm grateful for those memories. We had our love and everything we needed growin' up. Unfortunately, it came along with some abuse."

"Was there drug and alcohol use on your mom's side of the family, too?"

"Yeah."

"Did you spend much time with them?"

"Not as much as my dad's side. When we were littler, like in elementary school and maybe junior high. I had a couple of uncles. We did spend some time with 'em. They would take us to like— My grandpa used to take us to the wrestling at the coliseum—the WWF. My uncles were into cars, so we went to the race track a few times and things like that. Car shows. We did spend some time with them. But on that side of the family, it was alcohol. Big alcohol. All of them drank their whole lives. My mom—she was a drinker. But she was a functioning alcoholic... So, yeah..."

"Do you think your alcoholism is genetic, or do you think it was being around family, and just having that sort of environment?"

"Well, I'm not quite sure if I inherited it that way. But I have a real strong feeling that I have that allergy where once, you know, you get goin'—your body just wants more, and more, and more. Because I've always been a drinker where it's all in. I've never been the kind of person where, 'Oh, I'll have a beer with dinner and go home and go to bed.' No, that wasn't me. I would stay up all night long and try to make it to work the next day—still high and drunk. Or pass out and miss work. That was my cycle. Both sides of my family... That was the norm—drinkin' and smokin' weed. That's what they did. That was the culture. So as far as inheriting it, I inherited the culture. Genetically, I think that's referring to the allergy. I think I got that allergy. Yeah...

"And what's odd is, anytime I would go to jail or whatever—before sobriety. It didn't bother me. You know, I never had the shakes. I never... When I was in jail, I was okay not gettin' high and drinkin'. 'Cause, you know, some people go to jail, and they'll look for— They'll look to buy some weed. If someone's sellin' weed in prison, they'll try to buy it. Or if someone is sellin' their medication—their prescribed medications, that they get in the jail. They'll try to sell 'em. There's people that try to buy 'em. I was never that kind of person. If I was in jail, I was okay. I didn't need— But yeah, as soon as I get started... it's on. That was my routine. That was the norm."

"When did you first start getting into legal trouble?"

"Oh shoot... The first time I got in trouble, we were stealin' stuff—snacks from a 7-11. I think it was sixth grade, during the week of the SAT tests.[18] It was the morning. We didn't have money for snacks. And they actually called the cops on us and took us to the station, for our parents to come pick us up. I don't think any charges came of that, but that happened to me in the sixth grade.

"Then growin' up, a little later when I was like sixteen, seventeen, eighteen—I had a high school girlfriend. And so, I ended up getting charges, because she had this thing against her dad, who had divorced her mom. He had a house up in the mountains and she wanted to go over there. And we actually went into that house when no one was home. And so, I ended up gettin' a legal charge for that. Yeah, Trespassing. Or whatever it was. I don't remember."

"How did you guys get caught?"

"The neighbors or someone. I don't know. The neighbors may have called the police 'cause they saw an unrecognized vehicle on that property, maybe. I don't know. But when we were leaving, goin' down the mountain roads there, we got pulled over. The cops were on their way to the scene when we were pretty much leaving, or whatever. So, I assume somebody saw

---

[18] SAT stands for Standard Aptitude Test, which is used to evaluate students for college admissions.

a car that shouldn't have been there—on that property. 'Cause it was like, the small neighborhoods that are tucked in the trees. You know, that kind of situation. So, I don't know. Shit, that was three lifetimes ago."

"Were you drinking and drugging with all that stuff? Like, can you attribute some of that stuff to being loaded?"

"The criminal stuff? I don't think so—at that time. To be honest, when I was with my girlfriend in ninth grade, I was probably drinkin' and druggin' around those days. But the day of? No, I don't think I was drunk or high or anything. Later, when I was eighteen, nineteen—because of drinkin' and druggin'—I was out breaking into cars with friends. And I learned how to do it, and thought it was okay and cool because that's what I saw my brother and his friends doin'.

"So, the first time I had gotten an adult criminal charge, I was eighteen, nineteen years old. It was all behind the use of drugs—trying to get money for drugs. Doin' the fun thing. You know? Bein' stupid. My friend was breaking into cars. I was the driver. But I did end up getting two years sentence out of county for the halfway house. And because of drinkin' while at the halfway house, I got regressed and went to prison for Felony Criminal Trespassing— 'cause we were breakin' into cars."

"That was a felony?"

"Yep. Back then, twenty-somethin' years ago, that was a felony. But because of my two-year sentence in the halfway house— I was drinkin'… After like four months, I got caught drinkin'. Then the judge converted that sentence to eighteen months prison—DOC. So, I went through that when I was nineteen years old… Yeah, for breakin' into cars."

"What prison did you go to, do you mind me asking?"

"When I went to prison, it was a minimum-security camp. I went to Rifle, Colorado. It was a work camp. But because I didn't have my GED and I needed to take drug and alcohol classes; I had a job on the campus there—in the kitchen. And I also went to my classes. And that's where I got my GED."

"Was that scary for you as a kid—nineteen years old?"

"Well, no… It sucked bein' away, and ripped away from where I was from… But I was fortunate. I'll tell you why…

"My brother, growin' up… He ended up getting into sellin' drugs. Big time. He ended up doin' ten years. He had gotten a ten-year sentence to the federal penitentiary for Drug Trafficking. And so, what I'm getting at is, the friends he grew up with, were also friends of my sister growin' up—when they were younger. But they were big, big time in sellin' drugs and stuff. So, when I say I grew up around this stuff, and it was normal… I mean, I'm talkin'… These guys… I grew up watchin' the guys do it. Big time. From the jump. I was already a frickin' alcoholic. Just a young, dumb, impressionable kid following suit."

"Because people on your dad's side of the family were dealing drugs, did you get into dealing drugs?"

"Well, no... It wasn't necessarily on my dad's side of the family. It was my brother. My uncle was a whole different kind of dealer than what my brother was doin'. You know what I mean?

"So, when I went to prison, one of my brother's friends—business partners, friend of family growing up—was already at that prison. When I got there, he took me under his wing. So, my first time goin' to prison, I was taken directly right off the bus, and he was sitting there waiting for me to step off the bus. I was fortunate in the way, I had someone looking out after me. Took me under his wing. I didn't have my own money, but I had everything I needed because he was there. You know what I mean? So, it made my time there a little easier.

"But it really... Bein' nineteen years old and just all of the sudden in prison for somethin'—breaking into cars... So, I had some resentments about it. I felt bad. But I made the most of it. That's what I'm gettin' at. I made the most of it. I got my GED. I did everything right. I got outta there as soon as I could. Unfortunately, when they let me out on parole, I ended up gettin' high some more and I had to go to inpatient treatment at a… It was like a two-week thing called STIRRT, back then."[19]

"Like S-T-E-R-T?"

"S-T-I-R-R-T. I can't remember what it stood for. But I had to do that at the end of my parole time because I was droppin' hot UAs for cocaine. My big thing was doin' the cocaine. I used to smoke. I was a visual get-high. I used to love making clouds. I used to love watchin' the smoke. Just doin' all that—the whole ordeal.

"Growin' up, at the ripe old age of fourteen, fifteen… When I told my sister— We were at my uncle's house partyin'. I was still just a kid. So, when I told my sister, 'I have a baby.' You know what my uncle does? My sister does? They hand me the straw to smoke off their cocaine foil. First time. I tell my family I have a baby… They hand me a fuckin' coke foiling."

"I don't know what that is."

"They would take cocaine, and baking soda and water, rub a little mixture on the side of the foil, let it dry and then burn the bottom side—and it would smoke. We'd suck it up with a straw. That's where I came from. So needless to say, I fuckin' ran with it. But that was my thing. From then, I was a coke smoker."

---

[19] STIRRT stands for, "Short Term Intensive Residential Remediation Treatment."

"That was your first time—celebrating the birth of your child?"

"Yeah, that was the mentality of the family I was raised by. Could you imagine the feeling that kid got from that coke foiling? And I liked it. After all the abuse of growin' up with my mom, bein' bullied by my brother, not havin' a dad. All the sudden, I hit that fuckin' coke foiling… I liked it. I was a coke smoker for years."

"It was that and alcohol? Those were your go-to's?"

"Alcohol and weed."

"When were you first introduced to the program?"

"AA?"

"Yeah."

"I think I probably did go to some AA meetings at the Rifle Correctional facility, way back then. I did a lot of Bible studies. I did a lot of that stuff. Fortunately, I had my roots growin' up. My mom had us in churches on and off. So, I had my faith, and… You know, so I was thankful for that."

"So, it didn't really stick."

"Oh no. Well, let me tell you a story. When I was in ninth grade I met my girlfriend—my high school sweetheart. She was two grades older than me. My first year of high school. And we both had eyes for each other. And around that time when I injured my knee, and I had my girlfriend, I discovered girls—if you know what I mean. And, uh, when I went to prison, I had already had two kids with her. Before I was eighteen, I had two kids.

"And while I was in prison, they were already a couple, few years old. And when I got out, I had to go to a hearing for child support stuff. And while I was on parole, payin' restitution… Just a young, dumb kid. Didn't know how to make money, this and that. Much less afford—on top of everything else—afford child support. So, I asked for a continuance—for the child support hearing. And the only way to get granted a continuance was to ask for a paternity test. And I just needed to buy some time while I was gettin' through my parole.

"Come to find out, the older one wasn't even mine. So, with that heartache, I went heavy back into drugs. That was my escape. That was my numb. The mom blamed me because the truth came out. I loved the crap out of her—the mom *and* the kids. I know that's a big player in me using for so long. And possibly why I started using again when I got out of prison the first time. I just numbed myself. Went to the moon and didn't look back for a long time.

"Needless to say, that didn't benefit me anything other than numbing my pain—living the lifestyle I was from. And it always being so easily accessible through my brother's friends, or others that I'd come to know over time. But my brother, he always did his best growin' up, to keep me away from living that lifestyle. As far as the selling and this and that—that group of friends he had. He kept me away from that circle even though we all knew each other, you know… And it hurt his and my relationship—as brothers. He kept himself away from me, too. So, I lost out on a big brother to the game—to what he was doin'."

"Was he part of a gang?"

"Nope. He wasn't in a gang. They weren't into gangs. They were just all about making their money. I don't know who they might have been in cahoots with. Or I'm sure someone somewhere along their path, and in their circle, might have been in some gangs. But I don't know. I never got into gangs."

"OK. I was just curious. Because I know for the other guys, gangs were prevalent in prison."

"Yeah, I don't think so. I never got into gangs. But like I was sayin', my whole family, bein' the knuckleheads they are and from the area… I'm the apple that kinda fell away from the tree. It's a blessing, to be honest. I'm the one that God chose to break the cycle… that had been part of my family in generations for generations."

"That's a huge success."

"Yeah, I'm grateful for all that."

"Have you had to cut family members out of your life now that you live in sobriety?"

"Well, my situation… It's a more complex answer to that question. As far as cutting people out of my life, there was really no one to cut out. So, your definition of… Like your thinkin' when you ask that question about cuttin' people out of my life— My mom's dead. My brother's dead. All I have left is my sister. My stepdad moved. He was the closest person I was, you know, closest to. I have family that… there's bad blood, bad history. So, there's family that I was already not talking to. Cousins. There's other cousins that I grew up with that sometimes I see. I didn't necessarily cut anyone out of my family.

"Anytime I want to go visit, that's no problem. They still get high. I don't have a problem bein' around 'em. I know they're high. They don't sit there and smoke and drink in front of me. But I can go visit and say, 'Hi,' and stuff. But it's not like we can make plans and go out and have a good day, or out to eat, or things like that because there's just… That's not what they do. They're gettin' high."

"There's no relationship there…"

"There's a relationship. We love each other. We get along. But like, to go out and eat is not what they're tryin' to do. There's just no common— You know what I mean? Nothin' in common, really. But we love each other. I can see 'em. I can go visit them anytime I want. As far as cuttin' anyone out of my life, I didn't have anyone in my life to cut out when I got sober. I was by myself. Talk about a lonely person... Yeah...

"When I came here, doin' the wrong things, I ended up stayin' here. Ended up on probation and never went back. And the only thing I had back there was my mom, who died. My brother... I tried to do everything I could as far as seeing him. I have my sister—the only one left. I see my kid when we get a chance—because our schedules. So that's really the only one I have in my life that I would have anything in common with. I've been single for so long, you know... There's nothin' like that. So... But I did [a] change in location. The geographic change. The places I hang around... That's what happened for me—was I came here."

"Obviously, that worked for you."

"Absolutely did... So as far as gettin' out of prison, I found myself in more trouble for Driving Under Suspensions. And I ended up getting another— I ended up getting my second prison sentence when I was twenty-three for Drug Possession.

"I was out all night. I used to sell a little bit of drugs back here and there. They tore apart the car I was driving. And they found a dirty seal with meth residue underneath the bench seat—the back seat of the car I was drivin'. And my public defender tells me, 'Take this plea deal.' And the DA agreed. 'They'll give you two years' probation.'

"I said, 'OK. I'll get out of jail.' 'Cause I was sittin' in jail, waiting for court.

"The judge goes, 'OK. You can plead guilty. But just so you know, I don't accept plea bargain deals. I'm givin' you two years prison.'

"So, the day of court, I thought I was gettin' out—on probation. The judge turns around, tells me news my public defender didn't tell me. I was twenty-three. They gave me a two-year prison sentence.

"Second prison sentence came from the same county. Yeah... So, I went to prison. I was fortunate. They gave me boot camp to try to get a good reconsideration deal—if I completed it successfully. I didn't go through it because... I told you I had a bum knee from high school sports. Not even two weeks into it, they had everybody do a physical. And because I already had in my medical records about my knee—during the physical the doctor told me I have an option to continue the boot camp program. But if I re-injured my knee there, I couldn't hold them liable for anything. You know what I mean? So, I decided to opt-out of the boot camp when they brought up this and that, and told me legally if something were to happen to me or my knee during boot camp, I couldn't— You know what I mean? So that was the situation there.

"So, I got outta boot camp. I went to a minimum-security camp again. That time, I went to Delta Correctional facility. And it was another work camp, minimum security, and I sat there for twenty-three months out of a twenty-four-month sentence. You know why? Because when I went up for parole, they granted me parole, but my parole plan didn't get approved. So, I had to submit a second parole plan. And by the time the second parole plan went through, over time—even though I got granted parole on my first parole hearing—I ended up doin' twenty-three months out of twenty-four months because I didn't have a good parole plan."

"Does that mean you didn't have a place to go—to parole to?"

"Yeah. I had my mom's house. And at the time, she was living at my grandpa's house. You know why they denied it? Because in the questioning they asked if anybody in the house had ever been in any criminal trouble. She put, 'No.' They found out my grandpa had a DUI decades previously. But because she didn't list it, they denied the plan."

"Gotcha."

"So, I got out on parole. Unfortunately, I was back to druggin'. I was droppin' hot UAs on parole, for cocaine. So, I went back to prison to finish my parole—six more months. So, I did twenty-three months, plus a year on parole, plus six more months inside on a twenty-four-month sentence. Because back then, they had that mandatory parole time. That was the last time I been in prison. When I was twenty-four, twenty-five years old.

"And during that time, I had another kid with another lady. Unfortunately, I was in jail. But we get along today… When I left the mother, I was drinkin' and druggin'. The mom was drinkin' and druggin'. Mostly drugs. She didn't drink that much. But she was a functioning addict. It was never acknowledged, back then, that she was an addict. But she used drugs, pretty much just as often as I did. Needless to say, it was an unhealthy relationship.

"But after I left, I pretty much kept my kid at a distance because I didn't want to be seen that way. I didn't want my kid around my side of the family, because we were all that way—for the most part. It was a parental choice I made. I had my visiting time. I'd visit. We'd go do fun things. But not on a normal basis. Nothing court ordered. It was just at our pace. Whatever. But now we get along good. You know? My kid can call me for anything and I'm here. I'm present today. My kid doesn't hold anything against me and understands why… We've talked."

"So, what made you finally get clean and sober?"

"Well, for years my mom had been battling with an illness. She lived with it for fifteen, sixteen years. And me bein' the knucklehead that I was—back and forth livin' at her house. Livin' at my cousin's house—here and there. Over five years ago, horsin' around, doin' the wrong things—I got in trouble for petty theft. And then I got another charge. I was riding a stolen scooter. I had an open container of alcohol. I had drug possession. I had drug paraphernalia. I was a habitual traffic offender…

"When I got pulled over, they charged me with all those things. I'm sittin' in jail, facin' all those charges—felonies, and some misdemeanors. Just bein' by myself, and after all the horseshit times I've been in jail for drivin' under suspension, or petty theft. And knowin' my mom was getting older and I couldn't be doin' this to her anymore. I knew somethin' had to change. And I had to change. I had to. I was sick and tired of bein' sick and tired.

"They dropped all those charges, except for two. I pled guilty to Motor Vehicle Theft and possession of the drugs—Controlled Substance. And then they gave me probation. And I knew bein' on probation, I wasn't gonna be able to leave the county. I was gonna have to stick around. I couldn't run back [home] and think I was gonna successfully complete this probation. And I knew I didn't want to violate probation because I was not goin' back to jail anymore. I was tired and done. I was forty-somethin' years old; my mom wasn't doin' well healthwise, and I knew it was gettin' close. You know? I knew somethin' had to change. Fortunately, I was sober for my first year before my mom passed away."

"Nice… And you did that in the program?"

"Yeah… I stayed here. I got probation. I had to go to the shelter— 'cause I didn't have a house. I didn't have any money. I didn't have an ID. I didn't have a social security card. I didn't have anything. I didn't have a driver's license. I didn't have a job. I didn't have anybody that could help me. So, I went to the shelter when they released me on probation. And yeah, I started goin' to AA."

"What made you go back?"

"To be honest, I think I started goin' to AA because that's where I was led. The people that I came across since I've been here and goin' to the AA meetings… Somebody—by word of mouth—was at the shelter and goin' to Narcotics Anonymous. And she's the one that gave me the contact info of the people that I could possibly rent a room in their house. And now I'm the property manager of this house.

"So, what I'm gettin' at is, I was led to AA. People were placed in my life. Along with my strong desire to stay sober, and be successful, and complete probation, and stay out of jail. So many things fell in place for me. And AA was one of the major players in that.

"I tell you what, I've been tellin' friends of mine—different roommates that I've had, 'cause we have a house meeting here periodically. We have new tenants who are just getting fresh on probation—new to sobriety and just tryin' to get back on their feet… What I'm gettin' at is… Just so many things fell into place. Gettin' granted financial aid to go to school. Actually finding somewhere to live with support. They literally took me under their wing and said, 'Fuckin' do… do your thing.'

"I didn't know if I was gonna finish school. All I knew was I could get financial aid and I could get a roof over my head. I was desperate. That's what I did. My landlord, at the time, used to live here in this same house. She asked me one day, 'So, do you plan on finishing school? What are you going to school for? Have you thought about how long you're gonna be here?' Because she knew I was on a waiting list for apartments.

"I go, 'I don't know. I'm just tryin' to make it through the day.' I didn't know what I was goin' to school for. I didn't know if I was gonna make it through the first semester. I didn't know if I was gonna make it through the first week. I didn't know if I was goin' to make it through probation. I didn't know if I was gonna remain sober. All I knew was I was goin' to give it my best shot because I had been given a hand up. I made the best of it. And so many things fell in line. I refer to them as 'God sends'. Blessings just fell in my lap when I needed them, as soon as I changed my heart—when I was in jail and knew I needed to make a change."

"So, since that time have you had any relapses?"

"Nope. I haven't had any relapses. I don't know how many meetings I made my first year of sobriety. I've been to a lot of meetings."

"I remember I met you at the Sunday meditation meeting."

"Yeah, that was my thing. I made meetings my habit, part of my routine from the get-go. From jump. From word one. If I didn't do anything all day long that day, I knew I was goin' to be in at least one meeting."

"What other suggestions, that they gave you, have you followed that have kept you sober?"

"I make it to meetings. Don't pick up that first drink and you won't get drunk. I know that just being welcome in the rooms made a big difference for me. I knew I could go there and be welcomed. That if I was in a meeting, I wasn't gonna be hanging around with the wrong people. I knew if I was in a meeting, I would be at least closer to the herd. Being around sober people was a game-changer for me. And you know what? For me—I've never had a sponsor."

"No? I was just gonna ask you that. Do you have a sponsor?"

"Nope, I've never had a sponsor and I don't know why. I know that through my time of sobriety and makin' the meetings and talkin' with other members—other AA people… I know that at different times when I have an opportunity to talk to somebody, I'm realizing that I'm workin' on a Step without it even bein' on my mind. Just in conversation, I realize throughout my day whether it be at work, or at school, or with one of my teachers—instructors. Or with my stepdad, or with my grandma, or with my kid, or with my roommates… At any given moment, in any conversation I'm in, I know that it's a good conversation and a healthy conversation because I made it a point to be around healthier people. I come to realize I'm working a Step. Or I'm doin' the AA thing just out of nature. Or just because that's where God has me at that time. Or just because that's where my mindset is now.

"I've been around a lot of good people with a lot of years of sobriety who actually work the Steps in the program. And I've been able to reach out to them in my own time when things come up for me. Or when I have stuff to get off my chest. I have, and I do. And then I also did a lot of NA meetings in the beginning. I haven't been to an NA meeting since before COVID—probably over two years."

"What sorts of things do you do for self-care these days?"

"I got a gym membership. Growing up, my mom always had us in the swimming pools at the rec center. I've always loved to swim. My uncle—one of the uncles that always had us partyin', when we were hangin' out at my grandma's growing up—he always had us go into the steam room at the rec center. And swimming. And so that's something I've always loved— is swimming.

"And so today, this last four and half years, I've had a gym membership. And because my knee problem—and I also have some other issues—I don't lift weights. I don't play basketball. I don't run around the football field. I swim. There's no impact on my knee or any of my joints. So, my exercise is—I'll swim. That's what I do. My self-care is the steam room. I can go in there, stretch and breathe. And I'll tell you what, if all I did was stretch and breathe... I'm proud of myself. And stay sober. But that's self-care for me."

"Does that bring you peace?"

"Heck yes! Goin' through the probation, the first year—I lost my mom the day after Christmas. I had to go to the jail to tell my brother my mom was passing away. And the day she passed away, he happened to get transferred to the Department of Corrections. So, I had to call him the day after Christmas, at the Department of Corrections, to notify him [that] Mom passed away. They had to have him call me later that day because he had just arrived—goin' through the processing. So, he wasn't even officially there yet. But that was the hardest thing I ever had to do, was go to the jail when the doctors told us my mom had two weeks to live. He was on his way to prison… again. All behind drugs and alcohol.

"I did that my first year while on probation—while going through my first year of sobriety, while tryin' to get through another semester of school. A year later, I lost a very close cousin to drinkin'. And then a year after that, my brother dies in a jail cell by himself."

"But after all that shit, now things are looking good for you."

"I got a degree. I managed to keep a roof over my head—pay my rent. I went twenty-six years without a driver's license."

"That's a long time."

"There's a whole story behind that."

"Tell me."

"I don't have any DUIs."

"No?"

"When I was sixteen, I got pulled over. I gave them my license. They took me to jail for a warrant—for a Failure to Appear. For a traffic ticket I didn't even know existed, because somebody impersonated me and used my name. I don't know if it was my brother or one of his friends that I had referred to earlier.

159

Because the shit they did… I think one of them used my name when they got pulled over. But when I was sixteen, I thought I was getting some kind of ticket. I went to jail for an FTA, and they gave me a ticket, at that time, for Driving Under Suspension.

"So, bein' young—a young father goin' to school, goin' to work, and on top of that, partying—I continued to drive. I picked up a couple more Driving Under Suspensions before I went to a court date to prove that I was impersonated and should've never rightfully been under suspension in the first place. I thought they would all go away because I was never rightfully under suspension. Didn't work that way. So, I continued to tack on Driving Under Suspensions. Over my whole time, I racked up thirteen."

"Well, it's better than thirteen DUIs! Right?"

"I know… Not one DUI. I had one speeding ticket when I was eighteen years old. No wrecks. I wrecked just myself on the dirt road once. No tickets were involved. I was drunk… But no cops came.

"You know I like my bikes. I've always been a big fan of road bikes. So, I rode my mountain bike. But fortunately, my stepdad let me work with him. I lived under their roof so that was my ride to work. But I didn't do anything with it. I fucking partied my ass off. If I had my head out of my ass from the day

I started doin' electrical work, I'd be a master electrician right now. But I'm not. I'm an accredited practicing electrician now… again. I'm basically starting a lot further behind than where I could have been. But that's okay."

"Well, yeah—with all of us."

"Yeah, but I've had my driver's license back now for over four years. I have a clean motor vehicle record.

"It took me a long time, since I got sober, to forgive myself for lashing out. For being stubborn. For not being a responsible person. For not growing up. I couldn't forgive myself. It was hard. Pickin' up all those tools to live life on life's terms in the rooms… It changed my life.

"I went to school to help change my mindset. Bein' in class and making it through each semester, and successfully gettin' good grades. Makin' it to my classes, bein' on time, askin' for help when I need it, bein' accountable in the house I live in, bein' accountable to my peers in the rooms of AA.

"Needless to say, after everything I've been through… my whole life—my confidence level… Any kind of confidence that I pretended to have through all those years while using, was fake. I knew I had potential and wasn't usin' it. I knew I could figure out how to get my drugs and alcohol. And fuckin' bamboozle my way through this or that. But goin' to school and getting a room, and pickin' up tools, applying some resolve in building new habits…"

"They're self-esteem builders."

"My confidence level is in a much better place. Bein' able to get my electrical license after bein' revoked for a two-year period. Havin' to be patient and wait for my time to come instead of lashing out. Or sayin', 'Fuck it!' Gettin' a case of the 'fuck its'. Or just goin' off and sayin', 'Fuck it! What's the point?' You know what I mean? I don't do that anymore. Today, I have patience, acceptance. Today, I know tomorrow's gonna be better. I'll be one day closer to this or that. I had a lot of wreckage of my past that I get to deal with—long-term wreckage of my past."

"How do you deal with that?"

"It is what it is."

"Have you made amends?"

"There are some places where I can't make amends. And there's places I have made amends. Today some of my amends—my only amend—can be changed behavior. Like with my mom, I know I put her through some heartache and some shit. And so my amend is praying. Repentance. Changed behavior. Nowadays, if I say something that somebody might be offended by, or have an issue with… If I feel like I need to make amends, I clarify with them right away—so that there's no ill feelings in between me or anyone. Today, I know I can go in anywhere. Nobody has the right to have any ill feeling toward me because I've been doin' the right thing—the best I can, for over five years now. That's my amends."

"How do you deal with negative feelings or stuff that you don't want to feel, without drugs and alcohol?"

"Practice to pause. I think for me there literally was a switch when I made a decision in jail… That's the simplest way I can put it—for me. Because I've been blessed ever since I got out of that jail. Even through the loss of family. Even through the setbacks of the probation, or with income, or with the car breaking down. It hurts when my sister don't text back when I want to say, 'Hi.' For some reason, when these things have come up over this last five years… I swear to God…

"Literally, there was a switch flipped. Because with everything, every brick that's been thrown at my neck since I got sober… I have not reacted in any way near the way I would've acted in the past. I shit you not. There was a switch flipped in me. I can't describe it as anything less than a 'God send'—a miracle. God picking me to break a cycle. He decided to break the cycle when he saw a change in my heart—my desire."

"Well, one of the promises is that 'We will intuitively know how to handle situations which used to baffle us.'"[6]

"Intuitively know… I'll claim it. I'll testify to it. I will testify to that all day. You just said it the way I was tryin' to say it. There was a flip. I had a change of heart."

"Throughout your life, how much time altogether did you spend in jails and prisons?"

"Shit. I couldn't add it all up. To be honest."

"What would you tell someone that's struggling, getting in trouble, hanging around the wrong people?"

"I'd say it's never too late to decide to change. You can do it. You don't have to do that anymore. Today could be the beginning of a fucking better life."

"Has it been worth it?"

"Oh man… I'll tell you what, today I have some hope for a better tomorrow. Today is a whole lot better than yesterday. What's that saying about a life worth managing? Today, I have a life to manage. And it feels pretty damn good knowing that I can.

"I don't know. Maybe it's because I'm older now and I think I'm doin' things right—practicing the pause. Today, I can kick my feet up and take a week off, and I know I'll be okay. I know the few dollars I have, I'm not gonna go blow. Because I'm responsible. I have a clear mind. I don't know exactly what next week looks like. But I'll tell you what, I know I'm gonna be okay. I know that God's gonna give me exactly what I need when I need it. You know why I can say I know? Because he's done it for me this last five years. Ever since I had a change of heart."

"That was your spiritual experience…"[20]

"And to be honest, I've had a number of them throughout my life. I shouldn't even be here. Whether I should be in prison, or whether I should be dead, or be out in the street still. I could have easily, easily—I don't know how many times…"

"To help others."

"That's why I am where I am today. This is part of my way of giving back—bein' the house manager here… This house changed my life. Simply by takin' me under their wing. Simply by bein' around like-minded people. Simply by havin' a safe place to live where they say, 'Do your thing! Finish school. Stay sober.' I don't have knuckleheads comin' in and out of my house tryin' to use me—connivers, and drug addicts and alcoholics surrounding me—like I did my whole life, growin' up. Today, I don't have to worry about bein' woken up by horseshit. I have eyes that see different."

"What would you tell young men that are still getting in trouble?"

---

[20] The definition of what AA members refer to as a "spiritual experience," can be found in the Big Book on page 567 of the 4th edition.

"Oh man… You know, the way I think…is a person can talk till they're blue in the face. I could tell everybody anything—all the right things. Just like I'm sure over my years, people have tried to tell me all the right things. But did I listen? Was I tryin' to hear it? It wouldn't even matter what I would tell 'em because if they're not ready to show up, suit up, tie their fuckin' shoes… You know what I mean? If someone wants to keep showin' up—like they say, 'Keep comin' back.'

"It's never too late to stop. You know, you can decide to get sober. You can make a decision, but you have to desire it. I tried to decide to quit a bunch of times over my lifetime. I went to the classes. I did this and that. I tried to stay sober, but I was still in the environment that got me into the drinkin' and druggin'. When I really desired sobriety, when I desired a different way of life, when I realized I deserved better… After a life of fuckin' in and out of jail—I was blessed. So many things fell into place for me. The new environment, the geographical change, the people that were 'God sends…' And I truly believe it's because— There's a quote that I remember from a book that I read when I was in prison… Probably twenty years ago. I still remember it to this day. Here's how it goes. It says, 'If I am not for myself, who will be for me? If I am for myself only, what good am I?'"[21]

---

[21] This quote comes from a book titled, *The Milagro Beanfield War*. It's the first novel in John Nichols's New Mexico Trilogy, published by Random House.

"I like that."

"What I was sayin' was, little nuggets I collected over all my years… Even though I was collecting all these nuggets—gold nuggets… Because in my mind… I spent my time in jails and prisons doin' the right thing—trying to better myself. Tryin' to get some knowledge. I decided I needed to try to do something. I made the best of my jail time. But I didn't desire it, so I always kept goin' back. I still kept goin' back to this, that, or the other. When I say you really have to desire it—you have to really mean it. Change your mindset. And only want to be around people with the same goals—the same mindsets. Or be okay with bein' alone.

"One big thing for me over these years is… I believe in the Trinity. I also believe in being sober—body, mind and spirit. When I finally desired it… 'If I am not for myself, who will be for me? If I am for myself only, what good am I?'"

FROM THE HEART

*"I knew that I couldn't live that way. I was gonna
die. My drinkin' and usin' goes to a place where…
physically, and mentally, and emotionally— Like,
there's nothing left of me."*

Something about the stark reality in his message, coupled with a genuine love for the program and its fellowship, speaks to me. Nick Zooms into AA meetings on his iPhone, joining us from thousands of miles away. Wearing wireless earbuds, he listens while ripping up flooring, running a circular saw, and taking trusses two at a time. Demolition work suits him well by providing a productive channel to expend excess energy. Though he calls his morning beverage, 'crack coffee', he claims it calms him down.

Along with online meetings, I've gotten to know Nick via FaceTime.[22] We talk about work, family, and how to sustain solid sobriety while wading through the chaos. Our frequent conversations usually take place as he navigates the tundra in an SUV. He shares shots of wildlife and beautiful backdrops—vicarious thrills for me. Lately, his camera catches newborn pups feeding in a roomy whelping box. Though the dog doesn't belong to him, labor came on his watch, and Nick stepped up to the plate. He aided the mother by assisting with five deliveries

---

[22] FaceTime is an iPhone video chat application developed by Apple.

during the hours before dawn. That morning revealed a man with rock-like features whose eyes glimmered with awe.

Back when Nick first agreed to participate in this project, illness kept him from his job. So, I wished him a speedy recovery. But selfishly, I saw an opportunity to interview him right away. As it turned out, COVID made me wait a couple of weeks. But Nick kept his word, and as soon as he could, he Zoomed in on his iPhone.

"Ok Nick, here we go… Are you ready?"

> "I can't see your face. I have, 'This meeting is being recorded
> by…' Let me hit, 'Got it.' OK, it's gone."

"So, what I like to do is spend, you know, a third— What it was like, what happened and what it's like now—a third, a third, a third. You can just go ahead and start, like you would at a speaker meeting, and I'll interject with questions. Sound good?"

> "OK, I'll do my best."

"I'm sure you'll do fine."

> "OK, so I was actually looking back at this. And so… The
> incident happened— I was arrested for Assault and Battery.
> Arrested thirty years ago. 1992. May 7th to be exact. Not that
> that day stays in my mind. It'll always stay in my mind…
> Exited—released in 1994. What it was like, was living hell."

"When did you start drinking?"

"Oh, when did I start drinking? OK, so my... The very first drug I ever did in my life, believe it or not, was PCP. And I was thirteen years old. So, then my first actions with alcohol, actually, was me and two other school friends robbed a twelve-pack of warm Dos Equis from the back of a 7-11 store. That was my first drink ever, and it was shortly— I mean, I was thirteen the first time I ever drank. I remember drinking three of 'em, only because they were warm, and it was gross, and it was very hot. And we were in a public park. And of course, I puked. Now, most people would think from a bad... from a bad situation like that, you know, that they would probably choose not to drink for the rest of their life. Unfortunately, not my choice.

"So, building up to— There was experimental stuff. I'm the son of a very successful military man. So, there were... There were times when I was just experimenting. But because of his own addictions—my father was an alcoholic. Because of my father's own addictions, there was not gonna be experimental processes for me to participate in—at that time. You know, smoking pot and, like I said, drinking. But that's what started it...

"At a very young age, I was put into a drug and alcohol program—a local program in San Diego, California, called Mesa Vista Hospital. Which... I'm really having to think about some of these things... So that was an extended stay program for— I mean they called it developmentally challenged children. Which you could apply multiple things. Even now—in today. It was ADHD (attention deficit hyperactivity disorder)-related. It was alcohol and drug-related. There were people in there, that were in there for their parents abusing them—obviously. Mental health participants too."

"Was it just you and your dad? Do you have siblings?"

"No, I— OK… So, I do have siblings. I have a younger brother. And I have a younger sister. Both, who are alcoholics. I am the only one— And it's weird because they both grew up with my dad bein' in recovery. But both of them are either too full of pride, or too full of ego, or 'don't have a problem.' But, you know, it says we don't pronounce anybody alcoholic. OK, well… they're both alcoholics, and they are both proud, and they are both full of… full of pride and ego. And they're too good for the program of Alcoholics Anonymous, which is unfortunate."

"Do you think you all inherited alcoholic genes from your dad—that alcoholism is genetic?"

"Absolutely. One hundred percent… So, I have actually been in four rehab facilities. Mesa Vista—twice. Mercy Hospital. And then, I was sent to a long-term facility—and I'll get to that in a minute—called the Brown School in San Marcos, Texas. I had ignited seventy-nine acres in Poway, California when I was on house arrest and not following the rules. And because of being young, and being on probation... I was escorted by the state of California with two sheriff's officers, both on— One on one side of me and one on the other. And I was escorted to the Brown school—San Marcos, Texas—in a straitjacket. Not real, really, really cool for a young child. At that time, I think I was... I'm trying to kinda draw a timeline for you too, though. So, I was probably fifteen going on... fifteen, going on sixteen. That was one of the longer stays that I was ever in. Again, because I broke probation and broke house arrest, the state of California was like, 'We need to do something different. We need to remove you from the situation. We need to get you out of here.' But you know, to be real honest with you, that was a vacation for me.

"Obviously, we blend in like chameleons. And I started getting these privileges. Meaning, I wasn't always having to be on the site, and I got to go out into the community. And of course, being a young child in a very college town—San Marcos, Texas—I met who I needed to meet out there, and slowly but surely... Then I was... I was dealin' ecstasy and MDMA in a rehab facility, amongst smoking pot.[23] Not really so much drinking there. I mean, I obviously qualify for an alcoholic— more later in life. You know, alcohol became a lot more prevalent. And as a matter of fact, in— And I'm gonna jump

---

[23] 3,4-Methylenedioxymethamphetamine, commonly known as ecstasy or molly, is a synthetic, psychoactive recreational drug. It can produce altered sensations, pleasure and increased energy.

all around the place here, kind of—a little bit... So as a matter of fact, when I first chose to come to Alcoholics Anonymous, shortly being released out of prison—at that time in Oceanside, California—Cocaine Anonymous was a big deal. But I noticed that there was a much bigger crowd in Alcoholics Anonymous. So there for a very, very long time, I would announce myself as an addict. And very adamantly say, 'I'm nothing like my father.' You know, 'He was an alcoholic.' Which is so far from the truth. Later in life, obviously, I know I was just in a tremendous amount of denial.

"In the beginning, I knew I was a drug addict for sure. And I didn't understand alcoholism in its entirety. Because a lot of my story, before 1994... Everything really involved— I mean, alcohol was always there, but drugs were more a part of my story than alcohol. Where my dad was definitely a heavy drinker.

"So needless to say, my whole school life was not... was not real easy because I was in and out of several rehabs as a young child. So, I mean, I graduated. But I graduated school with a GED. I was in a regular high school for... maybe six and a half months... Yeah, maybe about six and a half months. And then, I went to a continuation school to further my education.[24] But

---

[24] The goal of a continuation school is to help teenagers graduate with a high school diploma, while working at their own pace and gaining vocational skills. Students typically come from high-risk or dysfunctional families.

in the continuation school, and being smarter than all the teachers, and everything else that I was doing… Obviously, there were a couple rehab stints in that, so. I mean, my schooling was so far delayed because of credits and stuff like that. But eventually… later in life when I decided to make a geographic— So I was a high school dropout. Just because I was lacking so many credits."

"You mentioned ADHD. Were you bored in school? So then, getting into lots of trouble?"

"Oh yeah. I liked to be the class clown. I liked to be the funny guy. I liked to be the cute guy in school. I needed attention and I wasn't getting it at home. The attention that I was getting from home—earlier in life… And I don't know when really— Like, what the breakdown period is. But I mean, my dad was an angry drunk. He was dealing with a lot of his scars from Vietnam. There was abuse. He was beatin' my mom and beatin' me. Never laid his hands on my sister. Growing up was very traumatizing.

"So, my dad actually got sober… And he had thirty-two years when he passed, which is really, really crazy. My mother— being very, very codependent—always worried about me and what was in my best interest. But basically, you know when my dad was in the military, my mom could not handle me—when I was a kid. And of course, it was easier to put me in a twenty-four-hour school or rehabilitation facility. The insurance carrier carried that. I don't really know how to say it. Like, they weren't trying to get rid of me. But at the same time, they couldn't handle the things that I was doin'. I wouldn't go to school. I was partying. Young ladies would be over at my house. Multiple relationships, as a child. Just really, really... a lazy youth."

"It sounds like you were out of control."

"Yeah, yeah. Alotta the times, too, in those rehabilita— They were experimenting with me with various, different antidepressants. I mean, as soon as I got out of those places, obviously... Well, I might of continued to do the antidepressants, but I was compounding them with drugs and alcohol.

"But so, yeah... A couple things that had happened— One time, under the influence of PCP, I thought my mother was a gorilla. And I grabbed the family home shotgun. Unloaded. But I didn't know. I was very much under the influence. There was an involvement with SWAT surrounding my home—my residence."

"When you say gorilla, are you talking about, like a—"

"Like, I thought my mom was literally a gorilla and was gonna attack me. And it was my mom. And it was just because I was under the influence of PCP."

"OK."

"Like I said, my story goes all over the place. When I get asked to speak in Alcoholics Anonymous, I have to put [together] little side notes. And unfortunately, I haven't been doing that for you. I feel like shit… But, best to describe it… You know, my parents did the best they could for me. I chose to go another way.

"So fast forward now… I'm getting out of this place that I was sent to, in Texas—and very, very mad at my parents. In fact, I wanted to be emancipated. I just blamed them. They did the absolute very best… So, coming back from Texas—I was not around my parents for very long after that. And again, that's when I dropped out of school.

"Then, at seventeen years of age, I left the family home and ended up in a relationship with a lady that was twenty-five. We had a place that was down in the beach—in Southern California. It's called Ocean Beach, which, we lived together. And of course, not feeling like I had love at the home, this twenty-five-year-old was giving me more love than I needed. I mean, it— Very, very explosive though. Because her dad was a cook for the bikers. And at that time, was making a lot of bathroom crank. And of course, we know how that goes. There really wasn't a relationship. It was a relationship of lust and drugs. Eventually, the relationship ended. I moved back in with my parents. We tried to work it out, but eventually, she cheated on me. Which obviously brought up some anger things, and not understanding. I was just partyin' and doin' as much drugs as I could continue to do."

"Would you say that you were loaded, like, the whole— 'Cause what I'm hearing is that you started doing PCP when you were thirteen. Were you sober at all during that time—back then?"

"Yeah, the only time that I was sober was when I was locked up. But if there was any way that when I was locked up, I could get loaded... I was. I would steal liquid paper and put it in a bag—in rehab—and huff it. Yeah, I mean, it's a miracle that I'm alive today.

"So, let's fast forward. Then, I got a crazy idea. I joined this thing called the California Conservation Corps because my drug addiction was... was just out of hand—with white powder.[25] So, I did join this thing called the California Conservation Corps. Their motto was, 'Hard work, low pay, miserable conditions, and more.' They sent me from San Diego—or San Diego County, basically. They sent me to Humboldt County. Which, I don't know if you know anything about California, but it's the Emerald Triangle.

---

[25] According to its website, The California Conservation Corps is a state agency, certified by The Corps Network. They enroll young adults, ages 18 to 25, for a year of natural resource work and emergency response.

"So, let's just switch from all of the white drugs to marijuana—
and probably the best marijuana in California. And of course,
[it] didn't take long for me to— And that's why I say that little
motto for them was, 'Hard work, low pay, miserable
conditions, and more.' So, what is a guy like me gonna do?
He's gonna, obviously, start selling marijuana. Which, you
know, in the Conservation Corps, I sold lots of it. I hate to say
it, but I did… I mean, people in there would jones so bad that,
you know, I'd rip 'em off. I'd sell 'em thirty-dollar, couple
nuggets—which if it were on a scale, it would be crazy. But
they were jones'n so much… Being up there though, I was one
of a very few people who had a vehicle. So, that was always,
'I'll fly, you buy,' type of scenario. It was a pattern in my life,
too. I just really always found a way or means of getting loaded.
Whether it was alcohol, whether it was pot, whether—"

"Do you think that was from pain? Do you think that started out early,
from pain—growing up in your family?"

"I'm sure it was. Yeah, there was a lotta trauma that like— I
really didn't. I mean, I swear to you, as I say this now. But I
really didn't grow up until I was forty-five years old. I lived a
lifestyle of… Just, so many different jobs, movin' all of the
time, just… wrecked relationships. I was always the victim in
them though, don't 'cha know? Thank God for the fourth Step,
and eight and nine—in the program of Alcoholics Anonymous,

today.[26] Because when I had to talk about my part... I've had very strong sponsorships that said, 'No dude. You played your part in those.'

"What was really interesting though, and what really kept me sober for a little while... However, I just kind of did what I know today is like—the one, two, three shuffle, so...[27] When I was released out of prison— Actually, the International Convention of Alcoholics Anonymous happened in San Diego, California in the same month. But I remember like, just this... this spiritual feeling, which I'll never be able to understand. But basically, there were— I don't know the number. Like, eighty-seven thousand people in the Convention—in San Diego Stadium. And they were sayin' the Serenity Prayer. And I was like... Even today, I can't even explain that type of message.

"You know, I knew it was a much better idea for me not to put drugs and alcohol in my body, because I lose control. And as a matter of fact, when I was detained—arrested and sentenced— I'd been high on crystal for probably three days. I don't know how much alcohol that I had in my system. Probably smoking pot, too. But basically, I assaulted a guy who made me feel really uncomfortable on the softball field. And it was my fault. I was chirpin' and drunk. Eventually, I took a bat to him. I

---

[26] The Twelve Steps of Alcoholics Anonymous can be found in the Big Book on pages 59-60 of the 4th edition.
[27] This is a reference to a pattern of behavior—repeating the first three Steps over and over to avoid the remaining Steps.

broke him up pretty good. I shattered four ribs. Severed his orbital. Both of his eyes were blackened. And he lost several teeth.

"And all I remember was it was happening so quickly. And like, people, after they pulled me away from him… 'You gotta go! You gotta go! You gotta go!' And of course, I tried to gather what I could together. But, you know, I was under the influence already. And I remember tryin' to drive out of a gate that was about a quarter mile down the road, which the softball park was inside of—which there was a barricade of the local Sheriff's Department. And I was detained. I wanna say that that was on a Thursday, and I was detained for the weekend. They weren't gonna let me see a judge on Friday. I was detained through the weekend. Then coming into pretrial, I admitted that I was guilty—which, I was sentenced."

"Do you think, because you were under similar circumstances with your mom— Do you think those things were drug-induced? Or do you think it was pent-up rage?"

"Well, if you want the real truth—today, I know it's fear. But sure, I hid behind anger and rage for a very, very long time. I was afraid of everything. I was afraid of life. And, yet to come—when I was incarcerated—was some of the most fearful days of my life. I wasn't a big guy. I wasn't a big guy at all. You know, I… Obviously, I had to fight in there—multiple times. I was told to do things that… that I'm not really gonna get into, just because they happened and I'm… They're in my fourth Step. But I just… There's things that I had to do inside of the penitentiary that I just—I don't feel comfortable talking about. Not because of you. I just don't…

"There were several things told to me by Shot Callers. You know, acts of violence had to be performed. I did two illegal things inside of there. But again, like… Being jumped inside of there, one time… I was in solitary confinement for ninety days because of an incident that happened inside. Immediately, when I got out and I got into general segregation—general population. I was only out for six minutes and in a dorm room and went right back into solitary confinement for thirty days. 'Cause somebody put some things out on me when I was released, and back into general population. You know, you either fight or you're gonna die in there. I mean there's no ands, ifs, or buts about it. I don't care what they do on television nowadays. They can't even, like… It's… But that particular period in my life is very dark. It seems so long. But yet, I look at it and it's short. But it seemed—"

"It's a lifetime."

"—like it was never going to end. I'd never been so nervous, so paranoid… the whole time that I was in there. A couple times, it's like… A couple times I— So I wasn't sober in there. I mean, there's more drugs in prison than— And that's scary. Various, different ways of making alcohol inside of there, that's just the most... Just gut-curdling stuff I could even think about nowadays.

"But you know, I definitely feel today, that I have beyond a gift. I have an ability, that it... With other men in life— Like, I don't sugarcoat stuff. I don't sugarcoat recovery today. I don't joke around about recovery. Recovery is everything for me today. And because of the Bible... Because of the Bible and because of the Big Book of Alcoholics Anonymous—I don't know the correct number of how many millions of people now have a lifestyle that is a gift. Especially the ones that choose to do the Steps of Alcoholics Anonymous... A simple— And how well do I fit into this? A simple program for complicated people... Perfect. I don't put anything in front of my sobriety... Today."

"What sorts of things do you do to protect your sobriety?"

"Lots of meetings. Lots of prayer and meditation. Sometimes doing a count—one through six—and walking away from situations. Sometimes realizing how important it is to be sober, and not have a reaction of mind that is unwarranted. Sometimes it's talking to other people—to talk me off of a sticky situation. And trusting God, that's for sure.

"I told my sponsor a couple weeks ago... I said, 'You know, all of this stuff that I'm going through with my child now. And how I am so raw with emotions... And being clean and sober.'

I said, 'The stuff that I'm dealing with—with the courts now...'
But now I don't have a Public Defender. I get to represent— I
get to pay for a lawyer. But like, 'The stuff that I'm going
through in this custody battle, just to be able to see my child—
is harder on me than getting sober, anytime that I ever got
sober.' I mean, that's why, especially lately, you know, I've
just been... having to reach out. But like I always say, I have a
disease that tells me I don't have it...

"Wednesday night, after work... I lost my conscious contact
with God. I lost my conscious contact with everybody who
knows and loves me. And... And I just... I wanted to act on
anger. You know? My anger is something that I've been
through multiple Anger Management courses. And all they
really do—and I'm not lying about this. All Anger
Management courses do is make you angrier. You have to be
guided through situations, which— You're basically dissecting
an onion. Like we say in AA, too...

"I have to really watch my anger. And when I got that terrible
news... Because once again, I'm delayed again for another
court sentence. Because I should rightfully— For the first time
the judge gave me the order, which is the visitation order. [It]
states specifically, that I am allowed to see my child during
Spring Break. Which, again, would have been March. And my
court date now is May 10th. So, she definitely knows what

she's doing and wants to push those buttons to see me react, or get drunk, or get loaded, or put my hands on somebody.

"But here's the bizarre thing… My record is expunged now. I am a free man. I was a felon in the state of California. I had a record back then. But because of what I've done, how I have changed my life, how I have become an employable man, how I have done what I was supposed to do. My record was— I don't even know the date my record was expunged. I don't even have the paperwork anymore. I used to carry it with me 'cause I was so proud. Like, I'm… I'm so free now. I've done my probation. I've checked in. I've pissed in your cups. I've done everything that I'm supposed to do. Now, I can possess a driver's license. I cannot possess a passport though. Only because of, you know, my child support order right now.

"And I think I owe her, like, nine-hundred bucks. But I'm not going to give her nine-hundred bucks to pay her attorney. Thanks to— And I hate to say this, and I'm not a political guy. But goddamnit, Biden's given her a lot of money, too. This child tax credit—money in her pocket. Every single stimulus that ever went out, went right to her. And those things were in my name. Not the child tax credit, but the stimuluses were all in my name—[that] she received. I'm just not… I still have a stubborn streak in me that is never gonna go away… That's just kinda me being a real douche with not just writing… But that balance, that I told—of nine hundred—started out at ten grand.

So yeah, she's good. But what we do have together is a child. I don't say that I'm sober today for my child. I mean, obviously I'm sober through and for the program of Alcoholics Anonymous. But my child... plays the biggest part in my sobriety, now."

"How do you handle other relationships in sobriety?"

"I have had a couple. Like, I mean, I'm gonna be honest. Relationships scare the shit out of me. I have not been in a true relationship since my child's mom... I've done some dating. But I really feel like I'm a relationship retard. There's gonna be so many things that I overanalyze in just being in a relationship situation, because my ex hurt me so bad by cheating on me, that I have not... And I've done a lot of writing. I've done a lot of praying. I've done the 'release of bondage'.[28] You know, and we're prayin' everything good for her that I want for myself. But I have not been able to have a relationship with another woman... Let me take this back. I don't think I will ever be able to love another female like I loved my ex. Because of the hurt that she caused in me and how many times she kept letting me down. There is a lot of hurt that has come from her... And I've met two amazing women. I just get to this place, where I just... I don't allow myself to go to a next level, maybe. If that makes any kind of sense. Because the next level would be all of those, you know... caring, loving, emotional..."

---

[28] This is a reference to a story titled, "Freedom From Bondage," found in the Big Book on pages 544-552 of the 4th edition.

"It's being vulnerable."

"Yeah. And I think I would be a great partner— I'm always a great sexual partner in a relationship. But then, when you gotta go to the next step and, you know—and you're really gonna talk about that 'love' thing. I mean... I can't explain what it does to me. I get scared. I'm fearful. You know? How could... What I really do is, 'Oh my God, if they only knew.' But like, I shouldn't block that from another... I'm doing God's work then. But I do it. And it's a character defect of mine. It's all over my shortcomings. And I'm praying to get rid of some of those, too.

"A while ago, I met a lovely lady. And I found myself in this situation that, she kept rehearsing into her past. Where there were certain things that I was reminding her of. And she knew my story about my child, obviously. And she kept going back there. And I said, 'You know what... Not telling you what to do, but I certainly think that you just put a Band-Aid over your own situation.' And believe it or not, me telling her that was healthy. Because you know, it takes two healthier parts to become a whole. And I felt like, I was ready to do this—choice. And maybe even eventually move in with her. But she was very much stuck on her past. And it started getting uncomfortable. I mean, the cool thing about her though, is we're friends. And we'll always be friends. So healthy relationships is what I strive for."

"Let's go back. Where were you first introduced to AA?"

"My dad."

"But when did you become an AA member yourself?"

"Hmmm… Well like, so when I was a kid in those rehabs. I'd get a little bit cleaned up in the rehabs and then I'd come out… God, it's so… I mean, when I was first introduced to Alcoholics Anonymous, I was, like, thirteen years old. 'Cause I'd go to meetings with my dad."

"At what point were you, like, 'OK, I'm done!'? When did you get serious about sobriety?"

"When did I get serious about sobriety? That would have been '07. And that's where I got several years up until 2015, when I relapsed."

"Tell me about that relapse."

"I knew that I needed to be back in AA, like, even after the first weekend I relapsed. But it was another ten and a half months before my current sobriety date—now. There were no legal consequences in my last relapse. But the guilt and the remorse, and just… Having to admit, and knowing drugs and alcohol are way stronger than me. Like, I knew all along where I needed to be, but I just… I'm an alcoholic and I'm a drug addict. I mean, AA seriously ruined my— And kinda good. Like, I don't say it in a bad way. It ruined my partying days for the rest of my life.

A belly full of booze and a mind full of alcoholics… We'll beat the livin' shit out of ourselves with guilt. And now, that's why my sobriety today is stronger than it's ever been. None of the Steps are half measures for me. None of them. Not a single one of 'em. And they're worked into entirety. And like I said, I make myself available to people in recovery and vice versa.

"You know, I often pondered and said words like, 'Man, fuck this! I just wanna get fucked up instead of dealing with stuff!' I don't even play with sentences like that anymore. It's not okay. 'Cause that, in turn, is like having reservations. And I cannot have any reservations about drugs and alcohol—period. 'Cause, I know. I've relapsed. There is nothing so bad that a drink or a drug is not gonna make worse.

"I don't get to hold out the 'normy' card. Like, I'm around it a lot, too. Even in my home now, with my roommate's drinking. Or sporting events. You know, when I start playing softball again, everybody will be smoking their pot, drinking their beer. And that's good for them. A couple times, too—I've said on a hot day, 'Man, a nice cold beer…' just like the commercials, 'would feel really good.' But I just don't play with it anymore, because I have a thinking problem. And once I think that it's gonna be okay… I just wanna make sure that I'm spiritually fit—well enough to not think in that manner."

"What was the turning point for you? Why was that different than any other time?"

"Well, 'cause I knew that I couldn't live that way. I was gonna die. My drinkin' and usin' goes to a place where… physically, and mentally, and emotionally— Like, there's nothing left of me. You know, I'm dehydrated. I'm pissin' blood. My weight is just… Like, I remember one—

"Oh, you know what? So, back this up. I'm trying to think of the timeline. But I mean, I was serious about recovery, too, in '94. I guess the strongest attempt that I would have ever made would be in 1994, because I didn't wanna get in trouble anymore. That lasted like, three years. And then I went out and I relapsed for like, seventeen months, or somethin'. And I drug my ex-wife—I drug her through the wringer. Eventually, we broke up.

"So, to answer your question—my first serious time ever, would have been 1994, when I was bein' released and I was in trouble, and I knew that drugs and alcohol were bad for me. So '94 was the first real attempt because I knew that I just couldn't… I knew that drugs and alcohol get me in trouble."

"How much time did you spend in prison?"

"Eighteen months. Eighteen months on a five-year max sentence. Eighteen months were long enough, though."

"Yes. So, I'm learning."

"Yeah, eighteen months was way long enough for me to experience what I had to see. And what I had to go through. And how much I had to… Just see a life that I would not wish for my worst friend."

"Was that a prison in California?"

"Yes, Donovan. Real close to the Tijuana border in California… multi-cultured prison. With the Muslims, and the blacks, and the Mexicans, and the whites."

"Was it segregated? Did everybody stick with their own race?"

Nick takes a swig of his Monster, and I watch him go back to that dark place he had alluded to before.

"Is that a stupid question?"

"Yeah, you kinda had to… So obviously, I went to a form of what was called the Peckerwoods. Basically, of like, neo-Nazi. We banded together very well. We stuck together very well. And there's just… There's a brotherhood. And it— You know, like I said, there's certain things that I don't want to talk about."

"That's cool. All you need to do is say that. That's good. OK… So, let's see, what's my next question—"

"So, what it's like today…"

"Tell me what made it stick for you? How did you claim your sobriety?"

"This time?"

"Yes."

"Let's go to 2016. That's this time. And this is where it sticks—now. 'Cause like I said, I threw away almost nine years of sobriety. I gave you that timeline. It was, like, 2015. And then I came back to the program... 2016.

"So, what stuck... is the fact that, uh... having all of the knowledge, all of the people that wanted to be friends with me in Alcoholics Anonymous— There's nothing so bad that a drink won't make worse... or a drug. And I swear—having a mind full of alcoholics and continuing to put drugs and alcohol in your body, is a nightmare."

"You mean recovering alcoholics?"

"Sure. And the faces... And the people that would call me when I was getting loaded before... Like, I would try to go to meetings, still. And even go to meetings loaded. And the thing that eventually stuck is, I went to that convention out in the mountains—in California. For the first time in ten and a half months, I made it from a Thursday to a Monday, without putting any drugs or alcohol in my body. Four days. And a convention. And they stole my keys. Son-of-a-bitches... And there was nobody—like, there was a store at that convention, too. And it was on a lake. So, I mean, they sold alcohol there. And they would not let me go by myself. I'm not gonna lie. If I was by myself, I would have went up to that store and I would have drank. I mean, I was hurtin'.

"I know that this is gonna sound crazy, 'cause like, I had attempted to work the Steps of Alcoholics Anonymous prior to 2016, too. But then after 2016… When I got… That convention—something about it was very spiritual for me. And like, I really believe—and I was three sheets to the wind for the next twenty-eight days detoxing off benzos.[29] 'Cause, I was eating six Xanax a day. Probably two to three 8 balls of cocaine a week. I don't know how much alcohol I was ingesting. I don't know how many gummies and pot I was… It was ugly.

"But that weekend, I had a spiritual awakening. I know I did. And I know it says, '… as a result of working these steps.'[30] You know what? No. I had a spiritual awakening. I knew where I needed to be, I knew why I needed to be, and I knew with the people that I needed to be. Then, the next step was to develop friendships. Which, the friendships that I have today are incredible.

---

[29] The term, "benzos," refers to a class of drugs called benzodiazepines, which are commonly used as tranquilizers. One of many uses, is to provide sedation before medical procedures.

[30] Some people interpret the wording of Step 12 in the program of Alcoholics Anonymous to mean that one must have taken the first eleven suggested Steps before achieving a spiritual awakening.

"Like, so here's just a complete fuck-up like me. And in the midst of COVID, these people throw a going away party for me. People were crying that I was leaving… That's unconditional love and friendships. And they would do anything for me in the world. What got really true—this time—is when I got back, I got two sponsors. I got a female, who was more of a spiritual advisor. I picked out another sponsor who… was part of CA (Cocaine Anonymous), but he was also an alcoholic."

"Is he still your sponsor?"

"Sure, he is. He's my good buddy. And what really happened is we got down to the meat and potatoes.

"When I worked my Step three with my spiritual advisor—in that conversation she reminded me that if I said, 'I know,' or 'but,' in that conversation—we're done working the third Step of Alcoholics Anonymous. 'Cause if you know—what are we doing here? Nothing will grow unless we have a foundation.

"So now let's talk about the foundation. What happens to people like us when we drink and drug? I don't know about you, but I'm insane. I'm a cheater. I've never been a thief in my life, if you can believe that, but I can become a liar. So, Step one is obvious in my life. Step two—what happens when we drink and use? It creates the insanity. Step three—Now I need to build a foundation. Nothing can be built unless it has a foundation. This is the bedrock of what is gonna create us as human beings, as people, as lovers, as friends, as employees. So, we have that chance as that foundation is built, we get to put the walls up. Those walls are our new character—our assigned character. As my God will have me today. So, now I have a new freedom. Like, don't revert back to the past. The past is bad for you.

"OK, then we get to the meat and potatoes. So now we're gonna write. And what I do with my sponsees now is, I give you six days to do your fourth Step. I don't want to hear any excuses. You have six days. 'Cause at that point, you will see how many new or different excuses… That's what my sponsor did to me. Pen to paper. Outline. It's not an autobiography. It's four categories. Go back, all you can remember… And then you have to share it with another member. You have to trust another person. And this is coming from a guy that was, like, 'What's your choice? Trust, drink and use, or die.' Well again, so now we've created that foundation. We're building our walls. Now, we're gonna trust—in the process.

"Six and seven is always gonna be part of our lives. There's certain things that we can pick apart… our character defects. My character defects have kept me alive. So, I'm not a saint though, either. You know? But I'm gonna work on these things, 'cause it's progress, not perfection.

"Then we get that dreaded eight and nine. I already told you the amount of people that I paid back. I have two that go on the second part of the ninth Step— '… except when to do so would injure them or others.' And I was freed. I did the work. It says, 'We must…' A must. Thorough… inventory. If we don't… we will drink again."

"And '… to drink is to die.'"[31]

"Amen… God is by your side every Step. God, your Higher Power. If you're atheist, I don't know what to say. There's a big reading about that, too.

"I don't regret my past, nor do I wish to shut the door on it. But I can't change that now. I know that I'm a much better man today. I know that I'm a lover. I'm not a fighter. Wow, did I just say that? I did… I'm a lover. I'm not a fighter. I am almost anybody's worst nightmare when my temper goes. It explodes. But I don't have to live life like that anymore. I don't hurt people today. OK? So, there's what the promises guarantee us.[6]

"Step ten, Step eleven. I get to pause, man, when I'm disturbed. I get to look through the channel of my day. What have I done anonymously today? And have we been of maximum service? Well, look at what we're doing right now. I'm trying to help

---

[31] This quote can be found in the Big Book on page 66 of the 4th edition.

you anonymously. OK, have I wronged anybody today? Not yet, but the day's not over. But I'll try to do my best.

"I'm told by my attorney to write something—to my child's mom. I'm gonna pray about it for three days before I do it. But, if I did it right now... Yeah, I could probably say a couple derogatory things, but we're gonna give it a couple days."

"Very smart."

"Step eleven— 'Sought through prayer and meditation to improve my conscious contact...' Amen, sister. I am— In my homegroup meeting. It is specifically a prayer and meditation meeting. We meditate for five minutes. A meeting to follow after. We have read the same frickin' eleventh Step... I don't know how many years. We read half of it; we share. We read the other half; we share."

"Out of the Twelve and Twelve?"[32]

"Yes. Yes, it's a great meeting on Sunday morning. I think I shared it with you... Those people love me—absolutely love me. And they know who I was... They knew... I was a referee a couple times in AA meetings, but nobody wanted to fuck with me. Like, people would start doin' dumb shit in meetings and not followin' the traditions. And of course, I felt like it was part of my meeting. I wasn't gonna let it get disrupted. So, who was

---

[32] This is a reference to the book *Twelve Steps and Twelve Traditions*, published by Alcoholics Anonymous World Services, Inc.

gonna be the first person to step in if there was gonna be an ass-kickin' contest?

"Oh my God, there's your character defect again, man. Just don't put your hands on anybody. I'm tellin' you what. I've seen… And I've had to tell men not to share the way that they share in front of women. Like, 'Don't degrade the opposite sex in front of me. Do not!' Like… 'You are here to be a part of something that is saving millions of people's lives. You have your opinion. I value your opinion. But your opinion might be somethin'… If you're gonna upset people at a meeting of Alcoholics Anonymous, your opinion might be something you might want to talk to your sponsor about. 'Cause if you disturb people in a group setting…'

"So anyways, character defect again. But again, I haven't put my—I mean, I've stopped a few of 'em. It just happens…

"And then we get to, get to Step twelve. And that's where it talks about, 'Having had a spiritual awakening as a result of these steps…' You know, when we get in front of our Creator and we're all alone, and it's just you and you. And you get that peaceful time to talk to your God… Your God is super grateful that you're doing the best you can for your sobriety that day. My God is super proud of me for not putting my hands on another male… That I don't put somebody near death. My God is grateful for me that I'm not out peddling kilos of methamphetamine and cocaine… so that gets into children's hands. My God is grateful for me when I am honest, when I am pure, when I am true. And my God is really grateful for Nick today, because I have nothing to hide.

"I will give the shirt off of my back for any man, woman, or child that I can. To let them know how important sobriety is for me.

"Like planning… How do they say it? I can plan, but I can't plan the outcome. So again, with the narratives that my attorney has given me today… I'm scared to death today. I'm running in self-righteous fear. I need to write a note because that's the judge's order. I must announce two weeks—to be able to see my child… I wanna see my kid.

"And furthermore, I do not, and I pray not—but I have no control of it. I do not want my child to be half as angry as I ever was. Because I didn't know what love was when I was growing up. I was abused—mentally and physically. I have never, ever, emotionally abused my child or physically abused my child. But my child has my genes… I want my child to know nothing but God and Love.

"So now you know. Now you know my story and you know my kind of rage. And you have a little bit of personal… kind of what I deal with here. But I am as cool as a coconut. And I've done my part. Now, what I do want my attorney to do, is to recuperate some of my court costs because that mother is in contempt of court.

"Another thing this program has taught me—be thorough, be sincere and be honest... and do my part. And I've done all of that. But I have another person on the other side that has done a lot of parent alienation. Said a lot of things that, uh— Like, I'm not gonna talk shit about people if they're not there to be able to talk about their side of things. I won't do it. For this circumstance, in particular. Like, you know what? Yeah, you can say, 'Your dad was a mad, angry... Your dad's been to prison. Your dad's been to jail.' You can say all of that stuff. But is that person the same person before we started building that foundation? You know, so you can't... You can't hold hate for what is in my past, because my past is— And that's why it's my past. Yeah, I did those things. But I have a plan and a course of life today that doesn't allow me, with the conscience I have today, to be able to do those things.

"All I wanna do— And I'm gonna, I'm gonna freaking melt when I get to squeeze my child. Like I like to squeeze some women in Alcoholics Anonymous. I am going to melt, like a little baby. Because... My child needs me... Because I'm not like my father. And the program taught me how to love another. How to be there for another. Unconditional love. I know in my heart today, because of the Steps of Alcoholics Anonymous, that I love my child. There's been many hurdles that are in my way. But you know what? I jump over 'em. You know, I may not always be happy about it as I'm jumping. But I'm gonna do what's suggested of me. And I'm not gonna control the situation either. I'm just gonna do my part.

"So that creates that fear. Because here I'm gonna have an attorney that I've been payin'. He's gonna present a case for me. She's gonna have a bunch of things that she wants to say. Most of 'em are hearsay. It is what it is. I know that no matter what happens in this, that my truth is gonna set me free. I already have a letter prepared for my child—that I had to rewrite four times. Because 'I don't know what to do anymore. My door and my phone will always be open to you. You may have to see through your own eyes—the truth.' Like, I have nothing to prove…

"But yeah, I have a life that's worth livin' today. I don't find AA to be as enthusiastic here as, A-in California, or B-doing the Zoom thing now. I mean, it's so diverse… Yeah, there's some good stuff out there. My Big Book sleeps right next to me—in my bed. In case, I get that alky… We don't really get to see it as much anymore—I don't wanna stereotype—as the chronic alcoholics. The guys that are gonna go into convulsions. If they don't have a drink, they are gonna go into either delirium tremors or convulsions. And you better bet that if I have to go do a twelve-step call, I'm going to give you a sip—before you do that.[33] Especially in my vehicle. You know, I don't so much mind if you're shittin' and pissin' all over yourself. That's part of this, too. I wish I could say I've never shit or pissed in my pants. I have. I can't tell you how many times I've woken up in vomit on the side of my neck. I believe in the way that Alcoholics Anonymous was, maybe kind of way back when my dad first started getting sober, too.

"But I like the angry drunks—because there's a way out of it. It's God. And it's okay to be angry. You don't have to act on it, though. You know, like, the biggest thing in Step eleven is— we get to pause. Like, my brain goes to bad thinking. But my actions don't follow my way of thinking a lotta times. And that has been my biggest gift in my life story. That's like, my biggest gift. I don't act insanely anymore. You know? And I certainly don't act insanely under the influence of drugs and alcohol anymore. Maybe Monsters once in a while. Probably 'cause I had a few too many. I don't know."

"What is it with you guys and Monsters? What the fuck is up with that?"
"I really like the taste of it."

"How do you keep your temper in check today?"
"I don't like that question."

---

[33] "Making a twelve-step call," is an expression used by AA members. It means to visit someone who's reached out for the help of Alcoholics Anonymous.

"It's gonna help a lot of people, if you can tell me."

"Well so, if it makes any kind of sense... Like, I will feel the feelings of full-blown rage. But I won't act on them."

"But how do you do that?"

"God! And sometimes it's so crippling to say, 'Look, I can see a bad situation's gonna happen.' I think something that is gonna be very good for me, too—and especially when my back starts feeling better—is for me to lose the 'man card' and get into Tai Chi. And it will be a commitment. And I think that it's gonna center my mind a lot more. And in that— Hopefully, I can learn to, you know, channel when I get angry moments. I mean, my life today, on a scale of one to a hundred... I might get angry fifteen percent of that time. My angry moments aren't angry days anymore. And I know that when I start getting like that— Now some circumstances we can't change, obviously. So as a human being, we are allowed to be angry. And of course, when somebody wrongs us, our immediate thing is—we're angry. If people don't follow their commitments, I get angry. If somebody lies, I get angry.

"For me... Honestly, I think that there only be two triggers—that I would lose my anger with—today. And that would be if somebody assaulted a female that I was with, or around, or close to. That would be a trigger. Or, if somebody hurts my child. Other than that, I mean, I deal with everyday confrontations, too. I have lazy people that I work with. That makes me angry. But, at the same time, then I need to step back a little bit and not have so many expectations to what I think they should do. Now should I pick up all their mess? Hell no! I should let them go down on their own sinking ship.

"But my personality is a little bit different, though. And sometimes, especially when I'm a boss, because I have people higher up than me. Their expectation of me is to get things done in a timely manner. Sometimes I come off a little, you know, little cross like, 'You need to get your shit together. You need to move a little quicker.' You know, I don't really have the ability to say, 'Otherwise, get on down the road and find yourself another job.' So, most of the time, and this is honest, eighty percent of my first thoughts are wrong. I deal with that. What has changed in that, though, is that those first thoughts are not acted on. And I will reach out.

"And yeah, I have a pretty cool life today. I like my life today. God's making the perfect woman for me, too. But I gotta stop runnin' from 'em, you know? I deserve to be loved today, just like anybody else. That's my own fears though. But again, I mean like, I don't go out and look for it. I do a little bit of dating. And obviously, it's a lot more fun to have dinner with lovely company. But, uh, I do what I'm supposed to do today. And I go into everything without having expectations. 'Cause expectations are nothing but a premeditated resentment. So, if

I leave my expectations at the door, I'm free to walk in that door. You know? We can't do God's work… Just for us to be alive today, is a gift—if you're a real alcoholic… or a drug addict.

"And that's just what I do. I hope that story helps you a little bit. Now you know who I am, and you can call me on bullshit. You won't hear bullshit from me though. My biggest character defect today is I'm a big ol' flirt. Just because I love to flirt. I can't help myself. I just… I mean, it's who I am. But you know, that's what is so dear. And that is my own line—that I have heard people come back to me and say, 'You know what, Nick? Just because you told me that you loved me that day—you gave me hope.'

"When I share at the end of the meeting, or whenever I stop talking—when I share that line right there, that is so true to my heart. Because you know my story now. And if nobody has told you they loved you today, I'm gonna tell you that I love you. And those aren't just words. That's coming from my heart. Because everybody has the chance to be able to feel that, too. And the only way that I did that was because of the Steps of Alcoholics Anonymous.

"Like, my fourth Step would scare the living shit out of some people. And then more, too, gets to be revealed. We obtain freedom through the Steps of Alcoholics Anonymous. How do we do this? We set off on a course of vigorous action. You know, you're not gonna get sober by osmosis, sitting in a chair drinking that whacked out-ass coffee in those church halls. It takes work… It takes work. And I love it."

WHO'S GOT IT BETTER THAN ME?

"OK, let me just put it like this, alright? Before the realization—

Funny money, plenty of honey, who's got it better than me? Nobody. I wasn't at the place where—who was I going to help have it as good as me? I helped people, always with an expectation of what I was getting in return. Not just what I was doing for them, but what they would then become responsible for doin' for me."

O n more than one occasion, I've considered telling John, "I appreciate your time, but I've decided not to use your story." Ironically, it's been his enthusiasm and encouragement carrying me through choppy waters—when moving forward seemed too daunting. This chapter, especially, has been a challenge. Our interviews were interrupted by incessant ringing from both his business and personal phones. He usually ignored them, but I had to stop recording several times so he could answer. Whenever I called, there were people in the background, vying for his attention. It was like competing with small children pulling at his pant leg. Other engagements demanded he be here and there, causing him to always run late—a mild annoyance, I've gotten used to.

Obstacles on my end only compounded my frustration. Disturbing "signs" caused me to question publishing at all. A few times, my cursor moved against my will—as if on a Ouija board. Transcription software couldn't convert the nuances of an East Coast accent, which added hours to my efforts. Certain translated sentences were cryptic and spooky. I almost gave up. And though this has been God's project all along, life's distractions kept threatening my finishing. Two forces have been at work—opposite energies, if you will.

In tackling this final section, I'm overwhelmed. The amount of material collected from five interviews with John has meant a lot of sifting. That there's more to his story intimidates me. So here, I've distilled his testimony—hitting highlights and leaving the rest for the next project. What follows is a sliver of his story.

"Got any questions before we start?"

"Do I have any questions before we start?" John looks to the ceiling in thought, then back at me.

"I'm going to be rigorously honest," he says. "You might cover your—" He covers his mouth and gasps. "[and say] 'Oh my God!'"

I throw back my head and laugh. After interviewing ten men, nothing could surprise me, right?

"Listen, the same things that might make you laugh right now, when you go over 'em, might make you cry. Let's put it that way."

He adjusts his shirt. "I'm ready."

"Why don't you start by telling me a little bit about how it was growing up—just basics to get us started."

"OK… I was born in Brooklyn. And at the time of my birth, there was a snowstorm. There was no way that my mother could go to the hospital, so she wound up giving birth to me in the house. My father and my grandmother delivered me. And, you know… Let me just tell you this. My mother—up until I was like eleven years old—she used to say, 'I could take a hundred kids like my Johnny. After all, he was homemade.' Later on, she was wondering how she could even put up with one of me."

"Are you an only child?"

"No, I have— I *had* five brothers and sisters. Two of my older brothers were killed."

"Were your parents— Did they drink and drug?"

"My mother—the strongest thing she ever had was a cup of coffee. And my father—whatever problems they had had when he was a younger guy, from drinkin', he stopped drinking. But I can remember gettin' pulled over, comin' home from Long Island. I can remember, back in those days when you got pulled over for drunk driving, very rarely would you go to jail. They would just say, 'OK, sleep it off.' Or give my mother the keys to the car and say, 'Don't give 'em back until—' Or actually, even go and get you coffee, and bring you coffee. That's really how it was.

"But in those days... my father and my mother, fightin' in the front seat. 'We got kids in this car! You're falling asleep!' Like, I remember that."

"Would you say you grew up in kind of a chaotic home?"

"Oh yeah, there was chaos. But it wasn't from my older brothers. They did their thing. They worked. They went to school. They took care of what they had to take care of. My older sister—she was always a good woman. My brother Richie—the worst thing he ever... If anything, he was a fighter. He was a hard worker.

"Remember the movie *Butch Cassidy and the Sundance Kid*? My brother Richie—he looked like the Sundance Kid. When he walked into a room, the older ladies—they just loved him. The younger ladies—they all wanted him. He lit up the room. When he was killed, I was in the Air Force. And I remember not wanting to go to sleep, because if I woke up it would've been, like... the reality that my brother was dead. I just wanted to believe it was a nightmare.

"Soon as I walked in the house, I remember... As soon as I walked in, my mother was just—she was broken. But she was like..." John stops, breathes deeply, and composes himself.

"So, uh… That was like the real, first, devastate— A lot of stuff had happened up until then. Like, a lot of things had happened… But that was probably one of the most devastating things that ever happened in my life."

"And how old were you?"

"I was twenty. It was 1981, so I was twenty years old… That right there changed the course… You know, I had been in trouble. Been in drug programs. I mean, I haven't told you, like… For me, at thirteen years old I got sent out to— It was just like, 'Look, he's gonna either get killed, or he's gonna kill somebody.' I was already stealin', dealin'. You know, just doing things that weren't safe for a thirteen-year-old kid to be doin'."

"Out of control."

"My brother-in-law, he was usin' me in ways… Like, he'd have me work for him and steal for him. Stuff he was supposed to be buyin'—he wouldn't buy it. He'd be like, 'Johnny, just put it on the dolly. Stack it.' What little kid is gonna be stealin'? But he used me like that. That 'Easy Buck?' You know what I'm sayin'? Like, what that wound up costing later on in my life. There was nothin' free."

At that point in his life, John was sent to California to live with his aunt and uncle. There, he attended a continuation school.

"My disease continued. I mean, I was in a school where people were naturally drawn to trouble."

He wound up with a cousin, who was a pastor in Agapè ministries. John remembers the day he was baptized.

"My cousin, he says, 'Johnny, come here.' And I went over by him. And then, him and his friend—they put hands on me. And he says, 'Will you accept Jesus Christ as your Lord and Savior?' And I accepted Jesus Christ as my Lord and Savior that day. And I'm gonna say this to you. I know today, I didn't always walk with him. I know for sure he walked with me. I been in situations—guns, shot at, thrown off buildings, killed in an automobile accident, prisons. There's no way, that's logical, that I should be sitting here right now, with you, and tellin' my story.

"OK, so… His sister—she's out there. She's just a wild child in California. So, she introduces me to her friends. And they were all continuation school graduates and non-graduates. So, me and this guy… All of the neighbors— It's a duplex or triplex. It's a summer night. They're all sittin' in front of their houses, drinkin' coffee, beer, whatever. Talking. You know, yik yakkin' it up. So, me and this other guy, we have this great idea. 'Hey, let's go in the back door,' of one of those families' houses. 'And let's rob them.' So we go in the back door, and we rob 'em. Me—I decide to take the guns. So, I take a rifle. I take a handgun. I put the handgun in my back. We got the jewelry, the money. Whatever it's gonna be, we have it. And now, we're exiting the place. But when we had went into the place, a neighbor had seen us. They already had called the cops.

"So now, here we are. We come out the back door. A helicopter is right above us. Now just think of that. I'm runnin' out the back door. I've got a rifle in my hands. I got another guy with me, and we're lookin' to get away. With that, we hear the sirens—police cars comin'. They have sharpshooters in the helicopter and they're telling me, 'Put it down! Put down the weapon!' Right? 'Put down the weapon!' And I'm still runnin' with a rifle. The cop said when I did this. I lifted it up like this, to put it in the garbage. He said the only reason that he didn't pull the trigger, was that the helicopter moved and took me out of his scope. And then, by the time I got back in his sights, the gun was in the garbage. And I had my hands up.

"Now the police came. And again, I got my arms up in the air. They say, 'Put your hands in the air! Do you have any weapons?'

"I didn't even answer whether I had a weapon or not. I was a kid! I went right to my back to pull the gun out of my—out of the back of my pants. And again, why was it that they didn't just shoot me dead? Why? Why was it, they didn't shoot me dead?"

That day, John was taken to L.A. County Jail. He describes it as a "rough" facility, where he had to fight throughout the entire two weeks he was there. Then, he was escorted back to his parents in New York, which was a whole ordeal in itself. But, for a variety of reasons, charges were not pursued.

"Wow... You're lucky."

"And that's like, what I used to think. I'm lucky. So, I'd go play a lottery ticket. Blessed—that's the truth of the matter.

"By seventeen, I can remember running down First Avenue in Manhattan. We had robbed a drug dealer. And he opened up the first-story window and he was shootin' at me."

Once again, John was saved from harm. Police found and arrested his friends, who were later released. Though they were involved, they weren't carrying anything when they were caught.

"Me—I've got the drugs, the money. And I'm just gonna, I'm gonna keep on, keepin' on. I guess I still had to get beat up some more. I had to beat up myself and people more before I actually got what was coming to me. Right?"

After graduation, John found employment in food service—working at a delicatessen and then in restaurants.

"You know, I was somewhat dependable. I'm not gonna say I was honest."

"Were you drinking and drugging this whole time?"

"No, I had momentary lapses of reason. When I got out [of school], I was drug and alcohol-free. I just wasn't character defects or shortcomings-free. You know what I mean? So, I worked. But then all of a sudden, it was like, 'Hey man, I'm working. I don't have to do the drugs. I could just sell the drugs!'"

It wasn't long before John was seduced by money and back into active addiction.

"I wind up with a connection—Ronnie. He used to get large quantities of cocaine from El Salvador. They're payin' like, average on the street—at that time—like, twenty-eight hundred, three thousand dollars for an ounce of cocaine. I'm payin' nine hundred dollars. Straight from El Salvador. Pure cocaine. Alright? I make an impact—you know, in this business. These guys are gettin' this coke, they can step on it seven or eight times and they're making money. It's that pure.

"Ronnie doesn't want to deal with anybody but me. He said, 'I don't wanna know your friends.'

"So, what happens is, I get involved with this guy, Anthony, who's an older brother of a friend of mine. He's connected with the Hell's Angels and the Pagans. He says, 'Listen, man, we wanna make a deal with you. We're gonna do three kilos—this stuff. You set it up.'

"I go to Ronnie. He says, 'John, I told you I didn't wanna meet nobody. I'll deal with you. I don't wanna deal with nobody.'

"I said, 'You gotta do this. It's three kilos. I'm gonna make a lot of money on this, man.'

"And, you know, he's like, 'The money—I'm not worried about the money.' This kid is smart. He's like, 'I'm not worried about money, man. I'm worried about bein' free. OK? And not havin' any problems.' But he folds.

"So, what happens is, we meet. The Hells Angel guy, Joe—he turns around as we're getting out of the car. He says, 'No, John. You stay here.'

"They go upstairs. They make the deal. Comin' down the stairs, Joe turns around to Ronnie. Pulls out a gun. And he says, 'Listen, you tell John that the deal did not go down.'

"Because what they were doin' is, they're gonna keep my profits from the deal. I was gonna come out with like, thirty, forty grand myself. My initial plan was that I would split it with these guys—on top of the table. That's how we do it. But they decided they're gonna keep all of it.

"Now, he gets in the car. Right? Ronnie sits next to me. Joe—he turns around, 'What, are you fuckin' playin' me?' He said, 'That wasn't the same shit that we sampled!'

"And I looked to Ronnie. 'The deal didn't go down, John. The deal didn't go down.'

"They drop us off. Ronnie just gets in his car and goes. He just leaves. He don't even say nothin' to me. He just leaves. And I leave. Now, later on, Ronnie calls me. He says, 'John, listen, man. The deal *did* go down. The guy pulled out a gun, and I didn't want to get us killed.' He said, 'I'm gonna give you what you should have made on that deal.'

"So now—ego, pride. I'm all that and a bag of potato chips. I call up Anthony. I say, 'Hey man, you guys gotta do me a favor. I gotta get out to the island, drop off a half a key. I'll give you the money.'

"Anthony comes and he meets me. When he gets out of the car, I pistol-whip him. I said, 'You can tell Joe he's next.' Right? And I'm an idiot.

"I meet Ronnie. I get what I think I'm supposed to get. I go out with my friends. I got all this money. There's like, six of us. We get mescaline. We're trippin', we're drinkin', we're partyin' with coke. All this goes on until, like, maybe six o'clock the next morning. Then, we're comin' down off the acid—the mescaline, and stuff. All of our senses are pretty much heightened. All the sudden, the door crashes open. And there comes this guy Anthony, [and] another mafioso guy. They come bustin' in with guns drawn. But the whole thing is, we were like, right on point. Like, boom! We grabbed 'em, with the guns. And like, we did it [in] two seconds. We got the guns. And I'm like, 'Oh, you wanted another one?' I start hittin' this guy again. 'You didn't get enough last night?'

"Then, I call my brother Richie. And I tell my brother Richie that these guys busted in. He goes, 'OK, just stay there.'

"So now, I'm holding 'em. I'm sitting in the living room. My brother Richie and his friend come, and they just act like they're cops. They put handcuffs on 'em and take 'em outside. They take 'em to the cemetery and they beat the shit out of 'em. They don't kill 'em, but they beat 'em real bad.

"Now, what happens is… By that night, my brother Richie—who, he's connected in a lot of different ways, with a lot of different things. He calls me and he says, 'Johnny…' He says, 'You gotta get out of New York. That guy—he's a connected guy. These are connected people. They're gonna kill you. I'm tellin' you to get out of New York.'

"There's so much to this friggin' story. It's just gonna blow your mind."

There's a promise to share more with me later. But for now, fast forward… John tells me about more crazy encounters with law enforcement, one of which led to a high-speed chase.

"For all the damage I did to their cars, [and] havin' my kid in the car. They really gave me a beating. I mean, I wouldn't say it was the worst beatin' I ever got, but it was one I'll always remember."

He holds up his left hand, showing me a crooked pinky. One of the officers broke it—a signature of the arrest. At the same time, another officer jumped on John's back. Unable to walk on his own, he was dragged through Middlesex County Jail. While there, his battered body suffered heroin withdrawal.

"They're gonna bury me under this jail." He told his mother. "You gotta get me out."

After six brutal weeks, on John's thirty-second birthday, his mother paid the fifty-thousand-dollar bond. Then, by way of lies, manipulation, connections, and technicalities, those charges were dropped.

Throughout his life, John was given incredible opportunities.

"Now what we do with the experience is really— That's the freedom of choice. That's why we have free will. And I'm gonna tell you somethin'. What I did with a lot of my experiences—I wish I had made better choices. I wouldn't have probably half the battle scars that I have… Physically. Emotionally. Mentally. You know I'm saying? Romantically. You know… Financially. Every one of those choices affected me, not in one way, but in every way of my life—at one level or another."

"Which specific incident was it that put you in prison the first time?"

"Actually, it was two incidents. They just got all grouped together. OK, one of them— I stole the car of a couple. And she had a purse. The credit cards were in the car. I went into Brooklyn. I used everything. I picked up somebody that looked a little like the woman and went on this binge—using her credit cards, buying all kinds of stuff, using the car. They busted me in Long Island. By the grace of God, I got out of that. I was held there for like, maybe a month or two months. But I got out of there. I don't know… It's in the records—how I got out. I don't know if I was bailed out or [if] they couldn't prove that I was the one to use the credit cards.

"While I was out, I had— I just was active again. You know, active in my addiction… I used to buy stuff and float checks. And then like, put the money in the bank before it bounced.

"So, what happened was, I went up to Pennsylvania and I got a truck from a guy who, we had gotten high together. I took the truck and the check bounced. And he went and reported it to troopers. So up there, what they did for a bounced check, you didn't just pay the bank back. They made charges.

"So, I went up there. I found out they had these charges against me. And I seen him. And I told him that, 'As many days as I'll spend in jail, you'll spend in the hospital.' So, they took that as terroristic threats. And they took it as transportation stolen—Stolen equipment over state lines. So, it became like, federal. But what they did was, they said—

"Well, there's a lot to it, OK... And that was my introduction to state prisons and federal prison."

"Alright. What was that sentence?"

"It was a four and a half that turned into nine. I did the full nine."

Later on, in his many years of heinous mischief, John landed at Graymore Rehab, a monastery in upstate New York that helps addicts.

"I get grounded in this place. I graduate with flyin' colors. Everything I was meant to do, I *did* do. I followed directions."

Once released, John seemed ready to make something of himself. He started what would become a successful business located in Florida.

"The name of my company is, All Phase Contracting. Hurricane preparation, hurricane restoration. Pavements to roofs. Everything in between. 'Why call anybody else when you can call All Phase? We do it all.' Alright? Within like, a year and a half I got seven trucks, forty guys workin' for me, three warehouses. I've actually become a millionaire. I'm worth a million dollars."

But change came quickly. John takes me back to 2005—a Friday night following a two-day drinking binge.

"I'm payin' the guys that work for me. I say, 'OK listen, tomorrow we got a couple of jobs.'

"'OK, John. We'll see you in the morning.'

"And I went to sleep. Sometime during the night, I got up. I got dressed. I went downstairs. I walked past the hotel desk. The manager—in her statement, she said, 'He was very personable, funny. He drove his truck right out of the parking lot.' No problem.

"I drove down to the Dixie Highway. I came off Iris Avenue. I made a left-hand turn. I had a head-on collision, and I killed two women. Well, myself and two women—we were killed in an accident."

John was revived in a flight for life helicopter headed to Florida's St. Mary's Hospital. There, he was put on life support and given a five percent chance to live.

"They said if I lived, I'd be a vegetable. They said I might be able to talk, but we probably wouldn't be talking about the same things."

Because of circumstances with other family members, the call to keep John on life support was made by his younger brother, who then began settling John's affairs.

"My brother made some decisions that— You know, he made worldly decisions, rather than spiritual. But that's resentments and realizations that I've gotten over already, and I've come to terms with. I'm not so mad or hurt of who I found out that people were—after my accident. I'm more hurt of who I found out they weren't. For a while after the accident, my question was, 'Why didn't I die?' And it got turned to, 'Why did I live?' That's what it's been. And that's what it is, today. I live to serve a purpose, today—the primary purpose. You know?"[34]

For weeks, I combed through material from our interviews. The original transcribed content was more than four times what I've included so far. Exasperated, I finally went to John and asked for another interview. But, this time, I explained, I needed a short summary of the pivotal points in his life.

---

[34] The final sentence of the AA preamble states, "Our primary purpose is to stay sober and help other alcoholics to achieve sobriety."

"Let's start with your realization—the realization you had that you were done [with drugs and alcohol]."

"OK… So, what happened is… The realization was, I woke up out of a coma that I had been in for six weeks. The nurse that was monitoring the machine, she's in the room—the life support. And I open my eyes. She goes, 'Oh my God!' Just like this." John cups his hand over his mouth and gasps, then— "'Oh my God! You were dead!' Right?

"I have a mask on my face. I have all the intravenous— I say to her, my response to her [was], 'Well, there's a heaven…' OK? She gets beside herself. She leaves the room.

"I wasn't aware— I didn't know how long— She came back in, and she had the surgical team that saved my life… The doctor was at the foot of the bed. The other doctors were disconnecting stuff, checking stuff. You know, adjusting stuff. They're looking in my eyes. The doctor at the foot of the bed said, 'Do you remember me?'

"Out of respect, I said to him, 'You look familiar, but I don't remember your name.'

"He says, 'Well, I remember your name.' He says, 'You're a miracle.' He said, 'You see this team here? We gave you a five percent chance of livin'. We said if you lived, you'd be a vegetable—that we might be able to talk to you, but we wouldn't be on the same page of a conversation.'

"He then, you know, did some other things. They disconnected some stuff, they put some stuff in, and they left.

"The nurse that was in there—she comes into the room. She says— Now, I've been in a coma for six weeks. She comes in. She says, 'May I hug you?'

"I was like, 'Yeah.'

"She comes over and she says, 'I just want to thank you.' She says, 'I've been a nurse for thirteen years. All of my friends are nurses, they're paramedics, they're emergency technicians, they're x-ray technicians, they're doctors. And I lost my father. I lost my father six months ago… And all I can think about is the things that we did, the things we never got to do. The things that we got to say, the things that I never got to say. And I've been struggling with his death.'

"She says, 'But my friends here at the hospital, they've told me about people. That they— They were in the room when they were— They had white light experiences.' She said, 'That never happened to me.' She says, 'I know… that that was my father speaking to me through you. And let me know… You were used as a channel for him to tell me that there is an after here. And that— It's really helped me.'

"I didn't know, yet, that it had been six weeks…I didn't know that I was only, like, a hundred and twenty-eight pounds. I didn't know that I had burned. I didn't know that my legs were crushed. I didn't know that. You know? —How many surgeries had been done on me. I just— I wasn't aware… of the tragedy that had taken place. I didn't know that I had killed two people. I didn't know that I had been dead and given a flight for life. I didn't know any of these things."

Few visitors came as John's healing process began. They were people he least expected, while those he trusted took advantage of the situation.

"I don't think anybody suspected— Nobody suspected. They didn't suspect that I was gonna survive this one. You understand? So, whatever they did, it was like, there wasn't gonna be any accountability. But that's between them and God."

At one point, when John woke up, a man was waiting by his bedside.

"He wasn't there to give me good news. He was there to get news. Alright? He didn't identify himself as a sheriff. He didn't identify himself as a police officer. He just started asking me questions. 'Hey, were you drinkin'? Were you druggin'?'

"I didn't answer his questions satisfactorily. I guess he had my record on, you know, being arrested—prison. You know, from before. So, he said— Just as he was leavin', he says to me, 'I hope you had a good time this time, John. Because you killed two women on Dixie Highway.' And he just left. So that's how I found out the tragedy of this accident.

"As soon as he said that I reverted back to who I was. I told you, I'm no stranger to the game. I checked to see if I was handcuffed to the bed. There was no handcuffs on me. I then, took out the intravenous, disconnected everything that was on me. I slid down to the end of the bed. And I was gonna do what I always do. I was gettin' outta Dodge. I was runnin'.

"When I looked to get off the bed, I fell flat on my face. My legs gave out from under me. I fell flat on my face. I really— I'd hit my bottom. I had to, for the first time, genuinely— I told you, I was always a pretty physical type of guy. Like, construction worker. I did for me… I had to [yell] 'Help! Help!'"

"The nurses came in and they picked me up. And from that time forward, a lot of people stepped in to pick me up. It wasn't always who I expected—[who] I thought they would be. But they were people that were there to help me. You know, genuinely wanted to help me.

"I'm not mad about who I found out people were. I'm more disappointed and hurt who I found out they weren't. And it's not somethin' that they couldn't be. It's just somethin' that they hadn't yet become in their own lives—what really matters. You know?"

There was a long period of recovery from the accident.

"There's still a lot of things that have to get done. I mean, you know, physical therapy… I'm just like— Acceptance definitely was not there. It wasn't the answer to all my problems 'cause I didn't accept any of it.[35] I wasn't gonna be like this."

On August 28, 2005, John stopped taking the narcotics prescribed to him.

"So, what happens is, now I'm goin' to meetings. I got people… You know, it's amazing. Because even, like, my family—my brother. They couldn't tell my mother what happened because it would kill her right there. Her Johnny. Who, she threw herself at the foot of a judge, 'Take me!' You know, it would've killed her.

"So, I'm at a meeting. When I leave the meeting, my girl—she called me. She says, 'John, there were sheriffs here at the house today. They said that you are a fugitive from justice, and you're

---

[35] This is a reference to a well-known quote found in one of the stories in the back of the Big Book. On page 417 of the 4th edition it reads, "And acceptance is the answer to *all* my problems today."

wanted for Manslaughter and Vehicular Homicide. It's in the Palm Beach Post. There's a ten-thousand-dollar reward for you.'

"Now here's the thing—my brother calls me. 'Cause I had been flying back and forth [from] New York to Florida. I was a fugitive from justice? I got bank accounts in two states. I got properties in two states. I got, you know, two cell phone numbers. I wasn't a fugitive from anything. This is what they were charging me with. I was like, how could I be a fugitive from justice? They gave me the flight for life. I didn't run. I was in the hospital.

"But then my brother calls. He says, 'Johnny, Mom is in intensive care. We just put Mom in the hospital. It doesn't look good. You better come up here.'

"This wasn't a thing of running. I was like, 'Look, I've gotta see my mother… before she dies. I gotta see my mother.'

"So now, I get up there… and I know… I know that my mother seeing me, although I was in a wheelchair… I was broken… She knew that I was fixed. My mother was definitely at peace.

"When my mother actually passed, people knew exactly where I would be. And the day of her eulogy, I kissed my mother goodbye, and everybody had to say goodbye to me, too. 'Cause

I got arrested. Mourners turned into Marshalls and they took me outta there. That was the first time in my life, I didn't resist arrest. I actually *took* the arrest. That word means so much. I had to tell my family, 'Hey look, this isn't about *my* arrest. It's about puttin' Mom *to* rest.' I knew in my spirit that I had caused so much confusion. And the peace that I had robbed her, and so many people that loved me, by the way I lived my life. 'Cause, truth be told, I was frickin'... I was hurricanes in Florida, and I was snowstorms in New York. I lived a life that was just, like, friggin' insane!"

A series of events took place—going through different judges and such. John was able to pay the half-a-million-dollar bond and got out.

"I had that afterlife experience where God, the Spirit of my understanding, said to me, 'You've repaired and built houses all your life. Now you're gonna repair and build the homes of the lives that matter. You're gonna open up the All the Way House.' All Phases Contracting turned to the All the Way House. It's not half the way, but all the way. It's not a halfway house. It's not a quarter way house. It's the All the Way House. Half steps avail you nothing.[36] OK? The cross was carried half the way, where a Samaritan was turned into a good Samaritan to help Jesus carry the cross all the way.

---

[36] This is a reference to page 59 in the 4th edition of the Big Book, where it suggests Twelve Steps to achieve recovery.

"And then He gave me this mission statement: 'The people that you're worried about sneaking around in your backyard. We could have 'em back there mowing the lawn and taking care of the landscape. That guy that you worried about kicking in the door, we've trained him to put in the door. Those guys that were looking in your windows, can now put in windows. We're helping to turn liabilities into assets in our communities so that when they're assets in their communities, they're gonna be assets to their families.' We were a place you could go, if you didn't have money, you could come.

"I wound up— 'John, you better take this fifteen years, or they could charge you individually—wind up with 30 years. It's the best deal.' You know, I got sold and told, and just… But the whole thing was, at that time, I had one greatest thing in my life—acceptance. Thy will be done.

"You know, I got a lot to be thankful for today—in my life. And that's why I do what I'm trying to do *for* my life. Answering the calling. And that calling is wherever it's heard. You know what I mean? Wherever they are, or wherever they be. That's where you gotta be. That's it.

"There's nothing more gratifying or satisfying, than just knowing that you've given yourself. You've used your most valuable asset—your time—to invest it in people's time. That hopefully they'll invest their time, and somebody else's time.

You know what I mean? It's not what you have in your pocket. It's what you have in your heart.

"So, in prison, I wound up being used. I wound up starting meetings where there was no meetings. This woman donated, like, five-thousand-dollars in Bibles. Every prison I went to, Bibles were sent to the chaplaincy department. So automatically, the chaplaincy department was callin' me. There was no diversion. I didn't get to get with this one or that one. It was like, boom! Right to God. Right to that channel for God.

"In Okeechobee, the prisoners would— We were separated. There was a fence that went down, and we had to be separated 'cause of different gangs, different levels of security. But we would meet out in the yard. And we'd come together. And we'd form a circle—a big circle—and connect through the fences as one. We would talk about the program—the Twelve Step program, God's program… Prisoners, but prisoners set free… 'Let it not be justified where we are by how we act.' What we really were, were prisoners of the world. But we're not prisoners in prison.

"To the day, they started this faith-based program in Belle Glade. Belle Glade was another maximum-security prison. I got sent to this faith-based. And I would have— At that time, I still had people from AA, people from the churches, people from the community. They were doing this time as I was doing this time. They didn't forget me.

"Now I wind up there. It's a faith-based program, but they don't really— There's a lot of, a lot of, a lot of bad things goin' on there, which I'll discuss with you, you know, later. But there's a lot of good things going on there. And I got, like, music equipment being donated, books being donated, AA literature, spiritual [books]. I got a lot of stuff that's coming in and I'm distributing it in the prison. So, like, I'm making a name for the program. Not for myself, but for what it is I'm involved with. It's just, it's happening. You know what I'm saying? It's just happenin'.

"So between, like, from Okeechobee to Belle Glade, there's this thing followin' me— 'Oh yeah, he's with the program.'

"And then the pastor, 'Yeah, we got Bibles sent here, too. We got this AA literature, too.'

"All this stuff is happenin'. I get in with the volunteers that are coming in, going out—the Kairos Ministry.[37] We start doin', like… They have record of 'em—different plays that we did. We did this play called, 'The Rag Man.' It got played in Belle

---

[37] According to its mission statement, "Kairos Prison Ministry International is an interdenominational Christian ministry that aims to address the spiritual needs of incarcerated men, women, youth, and their families."

Glade. It got played in the next prison I went to. It was that powerful... How God was working—how our Higher Power was doing His thing.

"I just thank God that I got involved. That I was bein' used as a channel to whatever capacity I could be used. I made friends with classification officers, inmates, gang members, ex-gang members, people in recovery, people out of recovery. It was just a thing. But it was always the same—the primary purpose. And just meetin' people where they're at. And helpin' 'em get to where it is that they're goin'. Hopefully, they'll start choosing the things that mean life and not death.

"So, Belle Glade. It became a place where I got involved with the volunteers that came to the inside, that were doing this stuff on the outside. And the big thing is, about that, [it] became part of my proclamation. Like, 'Look, man. When you get out, those people that came in—get connected with them when you're outside. You know, the disease is waiting there with open arms. But you also got people who really love you. They *showed* that they loved you with open arms.' So again—a choice.

"Again and again, up until when they actually closed Belle Glade, there's a whole thing that went on with that. There was so much robbery, thievery. The feds came in. They closed it down. Officers were bringing drugs in for the guys in there to sell drugs. They were gettin' paid. The people were gettin' played. And it just went on and on and on. They finally closed it. But before they close it, this TUMI class—The Urban Ministry Institute—was a program that, ninety prisoners were gonna get chosen—out of the hundred thousand inmates in Florida—to be part of this Urban Ministry Institute, which was to turn prisoners into preachers. And by the grace of God, I was chosen for that class.

"We were doing the classes, and then it came to the end. It came to the end where the prison was bein' closed. Where were they gonna put us? This program— Chuck Colson.[38] He went to prison, and he had this vision. He had a spiritual awakening. Chuck Colson was his name. Chuck Colson. You can Google that name. Chuck Colson. He's the founder of the Prison Ministry. Alright? And they didn't give up. They were like, 'This class that was started is going to be completed.' And as it turned out, a private institution—South Bay Correctional Facility—took us.

"So here we were—ninety inmates. We were transferred to South Bay Correctional Facility. And they donated one whole unit that housed ninety inmates. And we were gonna be in two— They supplied computers. We were gonna be in college

---

[38] Chuck Colson was an attorney and political advisor to President Nixon. Colson was indicted and served time in federal prison for Watergate-related charges. Later, he became an evangelical Christian and founded the Prison Fellowship—now, the world's largest non-profit Christian organization, helping prisoners, former prisoners, and their families.

classes for two years. Just studying. Studying, learning to live The Word that we were professing. I used that ministry to also import the AA ministry. And we did the same plays in that prison that we had done in other prisons. So, we were becoming, 'Confirmed'. You know?

"'Oh yeah, they did that here.' Or, 'I worked at Belle Glade before they closed it down and they made all those arrests. I know this guy. I know this TUMI class. These guys are good.'

"So now, we get there. What happens is, where they had one meeting, maybe—I get five meetings started there. We're havin' five meetings. I bring in the Back to Basics class— Wally Paton.[39] Wally Paton comes and does this whole demonstration for the inmates, the officers, and just… Great stuff is takin' place. It's just, this is happenin'. The All the Way Houses are still open on the outside. There's people— There's guys that are in prison that— You know, they're making a way for them. For when they get out of prison, to go into the All the Way House.

"Look, as much as it could have been done, wasn't done because the enemy stepped in. The enemy stepped in and changed the original format—the cornerstone that it was

---

[39] Wally P. authored the recovery book titled, *Back to Basics - The Alcoholics Anonymous Beginners Meetings*, published by Faith With Works Publishing Company.

founded on. You know? Like… I don't say it with ego or pride, but I'm gonna tell you. When I had to step out of my shoes there—in the free world, there was nobody there to step into those shoes. OK? The primary purpose got questioned. The primary purpose became more about the pocket. All about me. Not about Thee. Crap happened.

"But anyway, a lot of great things happen in South Bay. Then at the end of that stint, I wind up— I get sent to—"

"How much time did you do—straight time?"

"Eleven and a half… All my time in prison?"

"Well, both."

"Both times in prison I got a total of, like, between twenty-two and twenty-four years in prison."

"OK."

"The last stint was eleven and a half."

"OK."

"So, they turn around. From South Bay, now, I'm going to— They're gonna start preparing me to go back into the free world. So, I go to a place called Sago Palm.[40] And the same thing

---

[40] Sago Palm Re-Entry Center is a minimum-security prison in Florida. It provides programs to aid inmates in succeeding in life once they've been released from prison.

takes place at Sago Palm. A lot of good things happen. These are people that are comin' to the end of their sentences. I'm there for a year. A year to a year. Before I got there, I got sent back to the Florida Reception Center. And the atrocities that I witnessed that were goin' on there, and the miracles that were goin' on... I'll tell you all about that later.

"So now, I get to Sago Palm—one year to the day. The day I get there is the day I get sent from there. And from there, I get sent to Bridges.[41] And at the place in Bridges, you're still in prison, but you have a four-foot gate that keeps you there. The food is a lot better. There's a lot more programs. As a matter of fact, it's programs from morning, noon, and night. You know, different services you gotta do. Job assignments. There's a gym. A lot of things are there. You either work in the kitchen, or the grounds, or the gym, assistants to the staff. Whatever it is. But it's a good program. It's called, 'Bridges'.

"Now while we're in Bridges, another miracle happens. A guy that was supposed to be doin' forty-five years, who was my first cellmate, people were praying on him before we left to Sago Palm. Guys that had been in prison at Belle Glade before they closed it—we got together. We're like, 'What happened to this one? What happened to this one?' That one was facin'

---

[41] Bridges is a pre-release re-entry program at the Arizona Department of Corrections. It offers a one-year discipleship class to inmates transitioning from incarceration into the community.

forty-five years in prison. The first person I see when I get there when— We had just prayed for him at Sago Palm. He's the first person I see. He's in the first bed. And it's my friend. And it's just like, 'We were just prayin' for you.'

"He says, 'I gave 'em back twenty-five years. And I just gotta finish fifteen.'

"What do you mean when you say, 'I gave them back?' What does that mean?"

"In other words, when you do the habeas corpus, what you do is—[42] Some people— Like, my friend had a forty-five-year sentence. He was able, through court, to give 'em back twenty-five years. So rather than gettin' forty-five years, he was just made to do fifteen years."

"OK."

"So, he gave 'em back time. And then... Just amazing... While we're there, James Allen, who was the founder of the ARC program.[43] He winds up bein' brought there. Not something that I did. Something God did. And he gives the ARC message. Then, Wally Paton winds up coming there—givin' a

---

[42] A writ of habeas corpus is a court order demanding a person under arrest be brought before a judge or into a court, usually for release unless it's lawfully proven that they should remain detained.

[43] James Allen is the founder of The Addicts Rehabilitation Center (ARC), established in Harlem. He served as executive director for fifty-six years before retiring in 2014.

presentation there. Now what happens is, Bridges is gonna be getting closed down. So, then we do this all-out effort—

"Are we recording right now?"

I'm looking down at a sheet of paper. "Yes, but I'm writing notes, too."

"An all-out effort to save Bridges. You know what I mean? Like, what we could do—raise funds, raise awareness... It doesn't work. They want this— It's state property. They want this property back. They're gonna use it for what the state wants to use it for. Just... Craziness.

"So now, what's gonna happen is... Dispersion again. These people that have been together are now bein' separated. They're gonna be goin' to different types of state-run work release centers. OK? Where, now you're gonna work for the state. They're gonna get paid. Any money you make, they get a percentage of it. They assign you to, like, sanitation—for the state. State fairs. You work for peanuts. They take half your money. Atrocities. It wouldn't be bad if they were givin' 'em what they should get paid. But they put them to work, like, cleaning up the highways, pickin' up— Subjected to all kinds of stuff. The water plants. Anything and everything state-run, they're getting state inmates to do it. They're payin' 'em little, and givin' less... That's the truth.

"A lot of these guys, when they're goin' out, they're bringin' drugs back into the work release. People, rather than stayin' off drugs, are getting on drugs. They're making extra money that they can't make, because what they're getting paid from the state—they're obligate. Just, a lot of crazy stuff goes on.

"So that's why now, what I'm— Eventually, I'm gonna reopen the All the Way Houses, so that when they get out of the work release centers, they get out of prison— You're gonna still have to walk the line, just until you get acclimated into being a free man. But you also know that what you're free to do, you don't always do, because it just brings you back to those prisons. You've created enough prisons for yourself on the outside, you have to go back to the ones on the inside. So, it's just this concept and this message that's going to— As we're doing it right now. God's puttin' in place for us.

"So, how it is now… is where we're at right now. My life is beyond my wildest dreams. You know what I mean? Because I'm not living in yesterday's nightmares. That's why my life is beyond my wildest dreams today. See how things just get put in place? That's why it is beyond my wildest dreams.

"You know, I try to silence the noise of the world to just live in the voice of The Word—to hear the voice of The Word—of the Higher Power of my understanding. I hope to be able to make a contribution—a contribution that's worth distribution.

Because everything we contribute individually, we distribute to everyone. And it doesn't matter what you do, how little or big of significance you think your life is, your life affects somebody else's life. Big ways or small ways, you know? It's not so much today, questioning, 'Why didn't I die in the accident?' It's more of like, a question of, 'Well, why did I live?' What I was meant to live for. Today, it's the program. It's seeking and finding God's will.

"That's pretty much— There's probably more that I could say about how it is now. You know, sometimes… it's not always rainbows and butterflies. That's for sure. But you know what? I've come to realize that even what the disease and the enemy means for bad, God means for good. Someone is always learning from our experiences—the right thing, or the wrong thing. You know the choice is what we do or what we experience that makes it right or wrong. I always say that feelings aren't facts. The only thing that becomes a fact is what you do with that feeling."

"What would you tell a young John?"

Our interview ends the same way it started—with John looking to the ceiling, while carefully choosing his words. "I'd tell him, 'John, listen to those people that love you. Listen to the people that love you. And recognize the difference between being loved and being used. And choose to be used for what you're loved for… for Goodness.'"

AFTERWORD

This book was born as a research project to better understand my grandfather. For years, I tried to reconcile his virtues with his dark side. Though he helped people that others wouldn't bother to spit on, he ruled our house with an iron fist. There was much whispering in our home—hushed explanations of his sometimes lengthy absences. As a kid, I was taken to one of many sentencings where the judge peered over his glasses, as my grandfather stood in his best suit. "Mr. Maccati, it's clear you have larceny in your heart." And so, it was another goodbye to Grampa.

I, myself, have never done time. But addiction kept me chained and relapse stole half my life. My grandfather passed during one of my sober stints. He was able to see me happy. Death came in his sleep, before he could tell me his side of things. So, with a need to know and a knack for writing I embarked upon this adventure. Now finished, I feel I've come full circle. I see my grandfather in these pages, showing me there's good within all of us. With most questions answered, I find myself standing at the shore of forgiveness. Thanks to all who helped me find my way.

—TJ

Made in the USA
Thornton, CO
11/21/22 12:09:49

eb1c990c-fc23-444f-bcb9-1d51bbf1ecfdR02